DEVIL IN THE DARKNESS

DEVIL IN THE DARKNESS

The True Story of Serial Killer Israel Keyes

J.T. HUNTER

Pedialaw Press

Contents

PART III: A Methodical Killer For A Modern Age

Copyright

THE DEVIL IN THE DARKNESS: The True Story of Serial Killer Israel Keyes
Written by J.T. Hunter

Published in United States of America

Copyright @ 2016 by J.T. Hunter

This is a work of nonfiction. The names of a few witnesses were changed at their request.

Cover design, formatting, and layout by Evening Sky Publishing Services

ISBN-13: 978-0-578-70996-3

Preface

Originally published on April 29, 2016, this book contains the first detailed account of serial killer Israel Keyes and the people whose lives he so callously stole.

Out of respect for their privacy, the names of some of the individuals involved in this story have been changed.

PART I: Hemispheres of Darkness and Light

"And no wonder, for Satan himself masquerades as an angel of light"

2 Corinthians 11:14 (New Int'l Version)

One

On a warm, windy morning heralding the hotter weather of the Vermont summer to come, Detective George Murtie sat hunched over his chair, frowning in concentration as he fought another losing battle against the never-ending paperwork that always seemed to find its way to his desk. During his 28 years with the Essex Police Department, Murtie had learned the importance of setting aside time to chip away at the continually rising pile of reports and other documents. It was a tedious task and one that Murtie never enjoyed, but as his career had progressed, he had come to accept desk work as a necessary evil.

As Murtie leaned forward to finish another case report, the shrill sound of his phone shattered the silence, startling him. Although usually annoyed by interruptions, Murtie welcomed this particular distraction as a temporary reprieve from the monotony of writing. He lifted the phone to his ear and found EPD Detective Morgan Lawton on the other end of the line.

Little did Murtie know that this apparently unremarkable call on an otherwise mundane Thursday morning would launch the most unusual case of his career, and one of the most extraordinary investigations in Vermont history.

———

Though he had nearly three decades of service as a police officer at the EPD, Murtie had not always known that law enforcement would end up being his life's calling. As a teenager, Murtie had demonstrated considerable talent playing the guitar, and he aspired to be a musician. He briefly attended Berklee College of Music in Boston in pursuit of a career in music, but in the early 1980s, he became a born-again Christian and studied for the ministry while attending a small, interdenominational Bible College in Florence, South Carolina. Rather than wasting his musical ability, he joined a gospel music group, performing at church revivals and playing concerts at area prisons. He also served as an associate pastor, ministering in churches and prisons through music.

However, his life's path changed again in 1983 after his wife, Linda, became pregnant with their second child and started having trouble sleeping at night. While out for a drive with her late one night, Murtie noticed a police car sitting in a darkened parking lot. In the silvery illumination of the cruiser's interior lights, he could see a solitary policeman sitting behind the wheel, talking on his CB radio. He had never considered becoming a police officer before, but the more he thought about it, the more the idea of being a cop intrigued him. He believed that it would provide opportunities for helping people, something that had originally attracted him to the ministry as well.

After being hired by the Essex Police Department, he was sent to the police academy to prepare for his new career. During his subsequent tenure at the department, Murtie worked his way up through the ranks to become a Detective Lieutenant and head of the EPD's homicide division. He worked long shifts and often worked overtime, the extra hours necessitated by his status as sole breadwinner for his family. In July 2005, he was selected to attend a special three-month program of study at the FBI Academy in Quantico, Virginia. When

Linda had emergency surgery for a colon resection, he came home every weekend during the three-month program to be with her.

Throughout it all, Murtie's Christian roots kept him grounded. Despite dealing with illicit acts or coming into contact with criminals virtually every day, Murtie never wavered in his Christian faith, a deep-seated belief system that forged his identity and shaped his daily actions. His faith governed how he treated people, exercising empathy for victims of violent crimes, but also being emphatic for the human condition itself, adhering to the belief that even suspects and those convicted of crimes deserve compassion and fair treatment.

George and Linda were both just fifteen years old when they met in August 1972 in Burlington, a short drive from Essex. Linda was immediately smitten by George's genuineness and humility, and she could not help falling in love with his kind, gentle, caring personality. Although George had developed a drug habit during his days in a rock band, after they dated for several months, Linda gave him an ultimatum: he had to choose her or the drugs. He chose her and proposed on Christmas Eve, 1974, telling Linda that he wanted to grow old with her. They married in a small Catholic church in Williston, Vermont, on March 8, 1975, Linda's eighteenth birthday.

George's parents had opposed the marriage, and many of their family and friends told them that it would quickly end in divorce. However, George and Linda's belief and trust in each other – and in God – kept them together throughout the years while many of their friends' marriages collapsed. Linda always credited their Christian faith, their commitment to each other, and their relationship to God for the strength of their nearly forty-year marriage.

George Murtie (FBI Academy Photo)

"A three-fold cord is not easily broken," she often recited fondly.

As George Murtie answered the call from Detective Lawton, an unknown man was calmly driving away from Vermont with a suitcase full of stolen items stashed securely in the trunk of his rental car. He was not in any hurry. Although the items in the suitcase had been taken from a house in Vermont, their rightful owners would not be reporting them stolen.

The man in the car was a hard-working small business owner and an Army veteran. He was an attentive lover and a doting father. But he was also something more, something sinister. He enjoyed committing violent crimes, and he relished murder most of all. Killing gave him an unparalleled high. It was his addiction, one which he could ignore no more than a drug addict could resist the need for a fix.

However, he did not kill quickly. He viewed the act of killing as something to be savored, just as one might enjoy a decadent dessert or bottle of fine wine. And his ultimate indulgence came from seeing his victims suffer as he controlled their final moments of life.

The man in the car was a new breed of serial killer, one who studied other serial killers and learned from them. He was a crafty, clever hunter, stalking unsuspecting victims while hiding in plain sight. And he viewed the entire country as his hunting grounds.

Two

M urtie served as supervisor of the EPD's Bureau of Criminal Investigations, and he supervised the department's Search & Rescue Team as well, but he was nonetheless surprised when Detective Lawton contacted him about a missing persons call. After all, such calls were not unusual, even in this cozy, northern Vermont town nestled between the Green Mountains and Lake Champlain. Much of the time, the supposedly missing persons eventually turned up without incident, never really having been missing at all. Indeed, they often went missing on purpose. But it would soon become apparent to Murtie that this case was different.

Lawton explained that he had responded to the seemingly routine missing persons call shortly after 10:00 earlier that morning. Diana Smith had reported that her brother and sister-in-law, Bill and Lorraine Currier, failed to show up for work that morning without giving their employers prior notice, something which was completely out of character for both of them. Smith worked with Lorraine Currier at Fletcher Allen Health Care in Burlington, Vermont, less than seven miles to the south of Essex and bordering the eastern boundary of New York. When she learned that Lorraine had not shown up for work, Smith immediately became concerned. She quickly phoned Bill's employer, the University of

Vermont lab department, to see if Bill knew why Lorraine was not work-ing. Her worry intensified when she found out that Bill had not shown up for work either. It was strange enough for one of them to fail to show up, let alone both of them. Growing ever more alarmed, Smith called the Curriers' home, but no one answered. When she found no trace of Bill or Lorraine after driving by their house, Smith called the police.

Bill and Lorraine Currier

Bill, 49, and Lorraine, 55, had worked their normal shifts the day before, and they had last been seen by various neighbors that evening at their house at 8 Colbert Street in Essex Junction, a small, incorpo-rated village within the Town of Essex. Rebecca Bushey recalled seeing Bill in the side yard next to the garage working on the gutters at approximately 6:00 p.m. Nancy Eldred saw Lorraine sitting at her backyard picnic table smoking a cigarette shortly after that, and Todd Bushey saw her in the yard around 6:30 p.m. Another neighbor, Pat

Godard, recalled seeing both Bill and Lorraine by their pool sometime between 5:00 and 7:00 p.m. Investigators later determined that Bill had been online on his computer browsing webpages for FoxSports and Facebook until about 8:00 p.m.

Within 45 minutes of the missing persons call, Essex police arrived at the Curriers' modest three-bedroom, ranch style home to conduct a "welfare check" on the couple. The responding officers found all of the doors to the one-story, white-paneled house locked and all of the window shades pulled down. While peering into a window on the south side of the single-car attached garage, one of the officers noticed that the glass window portion of a door leading from the garage to the kitchen appeared to have been shattered as if someone had forcibly entered the house.

Looking into the kitchen, the officers saw shards of broken glass spread far onto the kitchen floor, a clear indication that the window had been broken from the garage side of the door. However, aside from the broken window, there were no signs of a robbery or struggle. Dishes and utensils were stacked in the sink, still dirty, but the rest of the kitchen was tidy. Bill's diabetic medication sat waiting in a shot glass on the kitchen counter. Lorraine's glasses and contact lenses, which she needed in order to drive, were also there. Bill's wallet was still in the house, but Lorraine's purse was not. Police later learned that a black, snub-nosed Ruger .38 revolver was also missing. Lorraine had purchased the gun for personal protection, a purchase prompted by her recent habit of listening to right wing commentators such as Glenn Beck and Rush Limbaugh.

Bill and Lorraine's beloved pets, their exotic birds, were in their cages in a back bedroom, and the cages were still covered. This raised more red flags when investigators learned that the Curriers always uncovered the cages in the mornings and never left their birds unattended for any extended period of time. Indeed, if one of them was going to be gone for long, the other would stay at the house to take care of the birds.

Shortly after searching the inside of the Curriers' home, police discovered that the telephone line running into the house had been cut just under the panel box.

Bill and Lorraine had bought their Essex Junction home in 2003 and moved there from an apartment in Winooski, where they had lived since being married in 1985. Bill joined the Army straight out of high school and traveled extensively both in the U.S. and overseas, serving as a military fireman, radio operator, and forward observer. He served four years active duty from 1980 to 1984, followed by two years as a reservist, earning an honorable discharge in 1986. Since his discharge from the Army, he had become somewhat of a homebody, preferring to spend his free time around the house, often perched in front of his computer. Lorraine was also a bit of a homebody, but she tended to be more sociable than Bill, and she loved spending time with her sisters.

The Curriers' strange disappearance spooked the residents of their quiet, suburban neighborhood in the small town of just over 9,000 residents.

"I'm nervous," neighbor Jennifer Roberge admitted. "I don't know about anyone else on the street. It's weird, I never thought anything in this little neighborhood would happen like that."

Roberge told police that her golden retriever had acted strangely around 7:00 p.m. on the night of the Curriers' disappearance.

"Very peculiar," she explained. "When the dog was in the house, she kept going to the door and she was just acting really weird."

Other dogs in the neighborhood had inexplicably started barking as well. Now Roberge regretted not investigating what had upset them.

"Maybe we should have paid more attention to the dogs' barking," Roberge speculated. "It was very unusual."

Another neighbor, Edwin Shipley, recalled how the Curriers had moved into the neighborhood after purchasing their home in 2003, and they had always been pleasant and polite. Shipley described Bill Currier as a "quiet kind of guy, but friendly enough," and noted how the Curriers had often hosted family at their house. Shipley voiced a common feeling among the Curriers' neighbors in reaction to their disappearance.

"We're all pretty perplexed about it," he said.

Pat Godard described the Curriers as a "quiet couple" who "tended to themselves, took care of their lawn, and had family gatherings." Although Lorraine did not approve of Bill's frequent internet purchases – he had a habit of always needing to buy the newest movies and electronic devices – by all outward appearances they seemed to be a happy couple who were "never harsh with one another." In fact, in the year prior to their disappearance, they had celebrated their 25th wedding anniversary.

Next-door neighbor Laurie Singer described the Curriers as "very nice and very quiet." They were, she said, "perfect neighbors." In fact, they often let Singer's children swim in their pool, and Bill sometimes mowed her yard. The Curriers had always kept to the same routine, and she never saw or heard anything suspicious at their house. Singer had gone to bed at 10:55 p.m. on the night of June 8 and had not heard anything unusual. Her husband, who had walked their dog past the Curriers' house at 1:05 in the morning on June 9, had also not noticed anything suspicious. Both she and her husband found the Curriers' sudden disappearance unnerving and "very, very strange."

Karen Tucker recalled talking to her boyfriend on the phone around 9:30 p.m. on June 8 when she heard what sounded like a gunshot coming from the direction of the Curriers' house. Her boyfriend had told her that it was most likely thunder, but she noticed that there were no storm clouds around at the time. The unexplained sound had so spooked her that she immediately locked all of the doors to her house.

Harris Quesnel remembered hearing a similar noise sometime around 9:00 p.m. that night. He figured that someone had discharged a rifle and did not bother investigating the noise any further.

Remembering how the Curriers always decorated their house and yard for holidays, Wendy James echoed the feelings of unease that plagued the residents.

"It's disconcerting and troubling because it's a pretty quiet, friendly neighborhood," she said.

At the University of Vermont where Bill had worked as a caretaker for lab animals, veterinarian Ruth Blauwiekel described him as a "quiet and unassuming" man who was always the first person to arrive in the morning and who "went about his business and did his work well." She recalled how Bill and his wife carpooled every day. He always rode to work with Lorraine in the morning and then always rode home with her in the late afternoon.

"I don't think anyone saw anything like this happening," she said nervously.

After Lawson filled him in about how the Curriers had vanished in the night, Murtie became the lead investigator on the case. Standing outside the Curriers' home later as evidence technicians began canvassing the site, he gave a frank assessment of the situation to a local reporter.

"It's a real puzzler," he told the reporter, "but we're treating the home like a crime scene."

From the moment he took over the investigation, Murtie was troubled by the strange circumstances of the Curriers' sudden disappearance, and he quickly suspected foul play. His gut instincts told him that the prospects of finding Bill and Lorraine alive were not good, but he never would have guessed what the case would eventually become.

Front view of Currier's House (Essex Police)

Side view of Currier's House (Essex Police)

Garage leading into kitchen (Essex Police)

Shattered glass in kitchen door (Essex Police)

Three

After ensuring that the Curriers' home was properly secured, Murtie contacted the Vermont State Police to request the aid of its Crime Scene Search Team, a specially trained unit that provided investigative assistance to local law enforcement throughout the state. Murtie shared what he knew about the Currier disappearance with the VSP and arranged a time for the CSST to process the Curriers' house.

On June 11, Murtie received a tip that a man had been seen driving the Curriers' Saturn sedan in the Essex Junction Shopping Center near Pearl Street on June 9 at approximately 1:00 p.m. The tipster, a former Tulsa police officer, advised that a vehicle backing out of a parking space almost collided with his car. The only occupant of the vehicle was the driver, a lone male. The tipster had not thought anything else about it until the media began covering the story of the Curriers' disappearance.

From the description provided by the former Tulsa police officer, investigators were able to put together a composite sketch of the man, a sketch which prompted dozens of leads from people who claimed to have seen him. Murtie followed up all of the leads, even though they kept turning into dead ends. He knew that even the seemingly least significant lead could end up cracking the case and, just as importantly, time was not on his side. The longer it took to locate the Curriers, the less likely they would be found alive.

After exploring several of the leads generated by the composite sketch, Murtie became curious about the background of the eyewitness tipster. He called the Tulsa Police Department and was advised that the tipster's credibility should be questioned. During a follow-up interview, the witness stated that he had been pressured into approving the composite sketch and had not really seen the driver very well. Based on the informant's credibility issues, Murtie deemed the sketch unreliable.

Of course, Murtie was not just relying on tips from the public. In addition to supervising the review of hundreds of hours of surveillance footage from twenty-five businesses in the Pearl Street area, Murtie orchestrated interviews of Bill and Lorraine's family, friends, and co-workers, monitored a canvass of the Curriers' neighborhood, and oversaw or participated in numerous searches of the surrounding area totaling 36 square miles in all. The searches were a particularly difficult task.

"When you search an area, it's almost impossible to rule it out 100 per cent," he said, the earnestness evident in his voice. "There's a chance we could go back and search some of the same areas more than once."

Shortly before 1:00 p.m. the next day, Essex police located the Curriers' car. The dark green Saturn sedan had been abandoned next to a dumpster in the parking lot of an apartment complex at 241 Pearl Street, just a five-minute drive from the Curriers' home. A cursory glance revealed that the driver's seat of the Saturn had been pushed back as far as it would go, and the passenger seat was pushed all the way forward. To allow a closer analysis, Murtie's team took the car and dumpster to the department's evidence processing site, and they began collecting security videos from area businesses in hopes of obtaining an image of whoever had left the car after parking it.

During a subsequent search of the Saturn, analysts found a piece of broken glass in the passenger side floor mat. The glass matched the safety glass that had been shattered in the garage door leading to the

Curriers' kitchen, indicating that the glass had been broken before the car was taken. This discovery cemented Murtie's belief that whoever broke into the Curriers' home subsequently took their car, most likely using it to abduct them.

While Murtie's team analyzed the Curriers' car, the Vermont State Police's Crime Scene Search Team was combing through their home looking for clues that might shed some light on their disappearance. Led by Detective Lt. Jean Paul Sinclair, the CSST members donned Tyvek crime scene suits, nitrile gloves, and boot covers before entering the house. After taking photos of the exterior of the house, Sinclair and his team made their way through a sliding glass door leading directly into the kitchen from the backyard deck. Sinclair inspected the shattered safety glass on the upper pane of the door leading to the garage and concluded that, due to the position of the broken glass pieces, it was unlikely that the door had been kicked in or slammed open. The crack lines in the glass remaining in the pane suggested that the glass had been impacted by something approximately 11.5 inches above the bottom of the window frame, slightly above the level of the door's dead bolt lock. Since the dead bolt was operated by a handle on the kitchen side of the door, Sinclair noted that the "hole made by the smashing of the windows would allow someone on the exterior side to reach through and unlock the dead bolt." On the frame of the garage side of the door, he noticed marks adjacent to the location of the dead bolt lock, indicating that someone had tried to pry open the door before resorting to smashing the safety glass. The flat end of a rusty crowbar hanging on the wall of the garage matched the marks on the door frame. After photographing the garage and house, the CSST took toothbrushes and shaving razors from the bathroom to obtain DNA profiles on Bill and Lorraine Currier.

Following some quick inquiries, Murtie and his men determined that there had been no activity in any of the Curriers' bank, credit card, or cell phone accounts since their disappearance. Surveillance video obtained from the Rite Aid located on Susie Wilson Road revealed that Lorraine had entered the store on June 8 shortly before 4:00 p.m., purchased several twelve packs of beer, and left at 4:05 p.m. The

Curriers had been frequent customers of the Rite Aid, located just a few minutes' drive from their home, but this visit turned out to be the last time either of them stepped foot in the store.

On June 13, nearly three dozen police, including officers from the Essex Police Department, Vermont State Police, and Chittenden County Sheriff's Office, conducted a search covering a one-mile radius around the Curriers' home. At Pearl Street Park, a search team formed a line and walked west through a wooded area until they reached Susie Wilson Road. A similar search occurred in a wooded area at the end of Gauthier Drive. Unable to find any trace of Bill or Lorraine Currier, Police Chief Brad LaRose expressed his disappointment.

"We are still hoping that the public will be providing some good solid leads," LaRose told reporters. "We have not had it yet. We're still piecing the puzzle together."

Lieutenant Robin Hollwedell articulated the feeling shared by the entire EPD.

"The fact that they've completely disappeared, none of it seems to make any sense," Hollwedell said.

Five days after the disappearance of Bill and Lorraine Currier, their relatives appeared before the media to appeal for the public's assistance in finding them.

"Bill and Lorraine Currier are kind and caring people, beloved members of our family," said Diana Smith, Bill's sister. "We are heartbroken by their disappearance and at a loss to explain or understand it. We deeply appreciate the dedicated efforts of the police in trying to solve this mystery and bring them home safely. We're here today to plead for your help in doing this. Please keep Bill and Lorraine in your prayers.

To avoid interfering with the police investigation, the family declined to take questions from the media, but concluded their remarks by speaking directly to their missing family members.

"Bill and Lorraine," Smith said, "if you can hear this, know that we all love you and we're doing everything we can to find you and bring you home."

On June 15, while the residents of Essex worried about whether they might suffer the same fate as the Curriers, a nameless man drove his rental car back to Chicago and boarded a plane to California. He spent the night in San Francisco, then caught a flight back to Anchorage, Alaska, putting over 4,000 miles between himself and what many would soon deem "one of the most disturbing crimes in Vermont history."

MISSING
Since 06-08-11

Have you seen these people?

Have you seen this car?

If you have any information please contact the Essex
Police Department at (802)878-8331.

Missing poster (Essex Police)

Four

On June 17, their concern continuing to grow, family members of Bill and Lorraine Currier gathered at the Essex Police Department to announce a reward of up to $10,000 for information leading to their safe return. This time Bill's mother, Marilyn Chates, spoke for the family.

"Please search your heart," she pleaded, "search your mind and review your memory and call the Essex Police with any bit of information, however small it may seem to you, that will help to save the lives of our dear Bill and Lorraine."

Chates provided some insight into the emotional toll that she and other members of the family were experiencing.

"We love them both with all our hearts. We're devastated by their disappearance and in fear for their lives."

Sharing the family's concern, and all too aware of a lack of solid leads in the case, George Murtie decided to request additional outside assistance. He contacted Special Agent Michelle Delpha at the FBI's Rutland, Vermont, office and requested a consultation with the agency's Behavioral Analysis Unit in Quantico. The famed criminal behavior unit always carried a heavy caseload, but an initial consult in the Currier case was scheduled for the earliest opportunity on June 21.

Although a couple of local criminals went missing around the time that the Curriers disappeared, Murtie soon eliminated them as suspects. The crime scene was too clean for the local thugs to have been involved.

A colleague of Lorraine's at Fletcher Allen posted on Facebook that "you can feel the tension in the air when you walk in," and an Essex resident posted about seeing missing persons flyers with a photo of the Curriers on the doors of rest stops along Interstate 89, adding that "this town is very freaked out, I know I am very freaked out. This kind of stuff doesn't happen here. I don't feel safe in my home anymore."

On June 21, Murtie and his team had their first consultation with FBI Supervisory Special Agent Robert Drew of the agency's Critical Incident Response Group in the Behavioral Analysis Unit stationed at Quantico. Murtie, two of his detectives, and three investigators from the Vermont State Police participated in the initial three-hour telephone consult with Drew, Special Agents Delpha and Jannie Emmons from the FBI's local office, and four other FBI agents from the BAU. The assembled team focused on developing a victimization analysis for the Curriers, including consideration of Lorraine's extremely conservative political views and Bill's internet activities. Following their first meeting, BAU recommended that Murtie and his team conduct an in-depth forensic analysis of the Curriers' home computer as well as their workplace computers.

On June 24, Chief LaRose met with the media to brief them on the status of the search efforts for the Curriers.

"Naturally as time goes on, we have an increasing concern that one or both may no longer be alive," he said.

"What is the likelihood that someone other than the Curriers may have been involved in their disappearance?" a reporter asked.

"That's a good question," LaRose said. "We just don't know."

"Can you at least tell me if there was evidence found in their car?" the reporter asked in follow up.

"There was," LaRose vaguely replied.

"That points to something criminal?"

"I can't comment on that," the police chief answered curtly.

As the days came and went, Murtie doggedly pursued every lead in the case that appeared increasingly unsolvable. He was hoping for something – anything – that might provide insight about what had caused Bill and Lorraine to vanish in the night. For seventeen long weeks, Murtie devoted the majority of his time to working the case, and he continued to hold out hope that some key piece of evidence would be found that could help complete the puzzle.

"Sometimes," he pointed out, "you don't know how all the pieces fit until you find one specific piece and it falls into place."

Still, Murtie was a realist. Although he believed deep down in his heart that the case could be solved, he recognized that the investigation was nearing a point of diminishing returns. More and more resources would be needed to make minimal progress. Getting national media outlets involved was becoming a real possibility. A feature story on *Unsolved Mysteries* could go a long way toward heating up what was starting to become a cold case.

On August 15, 2011, Bob Drew provided his Criminal Investigative Analysis based on information supplied by the EPD and Vermont State Police during their telephone consultations on June 21 and July 22.

Drew's analysis detailed the circumstances leading up to the Curriers' disappearance, including a description of Bill and Lorraine's backgrounds. Drew noted that Bill had worked at the University of Vermont laboratory since 1986, a position in which he was considered to be a "punctual, reliable, and competent worker," and in which he was "liked by his co-workers but quiet and reserved." The report described Lorraine as "quiet and compassionate," although she had "become very politically outspoken and opinionated" in recent years after becoming a fan of Glenn Beck and Rush Limbaugh. The report also noted that Bill was Lorraine's second husband, and that her first husband, who had physically abused her, committed suicide after their divorce.

Based on their background and activities, Drew opined that Bill and Lorraine had a "low to moderate risk of becoming victims of violent crime." The highest sources of risk for them were Bill's internet activities and Lorraine's vocalization of her extreme right-wing political opinions.

Drew's report concluded that the Curriers were now likely deceased, that they were abducted and killed by a white male, acting alone, using a firearm, that the offender had prior contact with at least one of the Curriers, that one of the Curriers was a "targeted victim," and that the motivation for the crime was "likely to be personal." Drew also opined that the offender "engaged in some form of noticeable post-offense behavior after abducting and murdering the Curriers," such as "increasing the use of intoxicating substances in attempts to self-medicate and calm" himself.

A central conclusion of the FBI's analysis pointed out that it would be almost unheard of for a couple to be randomly abducted from their home by strangers. The FBI recommended that the Essex investigators learn everything possible about the Curriers and their lifestyle so that a clearer picture might develop as to a possible suspect in their abduction.

Murtie heeded the FBI's advice, accumulating reams of information about the Curriers' personal lives and developing a timeline of their daily activities back to the beginning of 2011. However, nothing stood out as a possible reason for their disappearance. Although there were a few higher-than-average risk aspects of the Curriers' lifestyles, nothing about them generated any positive leads.

The BAU's report reinforced Murtie's own belief that Bill and Lorraine Currier had been killed shortly after their abduction. However, that did little to alleviate the frustration of knowing that he was no closer to naming a suspect for their apparent murder, nor did it quiet his growing doubt that the Curriers' bodies would ever be found.

On October 25, Murtie led another search for signs of the Curriers, the tenth and largest one to date involving nearly three dozen law enforcement personnel. This latest search came on the heels of an analysis of records subpoenaed from Verizon, the Curriers' cell phone provider, records which had been requested in the early stages of the investigation but had only recently been fully provided.

The Verizon records revealed that at 7:27 a.m. on the morning of the Curriers' disappearance, their cell phone received an incoming call from Burlington. Although no one had answered the call, it rang long enough for the signal to be picked up by a cell phone tower in Fort Ethan Allen in Essex. With assistance from the FBI, Murtie and his team were able to triangulate an area around that cell phone tower to lay out the boundaries for the new search. With so many boots on the ground, the investigators were able to blanket a location spanning from Whitcomb Farm to the area known as the "68 Acres" in Essex, partially abutting State Road 15 across from Fort Ethan Allen, and including the Woodside Juvenile Detention Facility, as well as surrounding woods and fields along the Winooski River. But the initially promising search produced more disappointment. The end result was the same as the prior ones.

"We found nothing," Chief LaRose murmured with an obvious frown. "It's disappointing on several fronts," he said gruffly.

And there would be much more disappointment to come.

Five

(February 1, 2012 – Anchorage, Alaska)

On a cold winter's night, a white pick-up truck pulled into the Home Depot parking lot next to an International House of Pancakes and Dairy Queen on Tudor Road. A shadowy silhouette in the driver's seat steered the truck into an empty parking spot and looked around. He spotted some security cameras by the IHOP, but they looked old. He figured they were run down and not likely recording anymore. Besides, he had his face covered with a makeshift ski mask, he had removed the front license plate from his truck, and the rear license plate was almost completely covered with snow. As an added precaution, he had also removed the green "Licensed – Bonded" sign and metal rack that usually adorned the back of his truck. Without the sign and rack, his truck blended in perfectly. A popular make and model with Alaskans, the 2004 Chevy Silverado was utterly inconspicuous. It looked like literally hundreds of white pick-up trucks being driven in the Anchorage area.

The dark figure sat in his truck for a few minutes, listening to a police scanner that he had recently purchased at Radio Shack. He planned on moving out of Alaska in the near future, back down to the

Lower 48, and he intended on getting a lot of use out of his new toy after relocating.

Agitated back-and-forth chatter squawked from the scanner, but it concerned something going on at the other side of town. The man in the truck smiled to himself. This was the distraction he needed. It meant there would be few, if any, police in the area he had targeted.

True to his normal practice, he had not selected his prey for any particular reason. It was the place, not the person, which he had picked. He had chosen the Common Grounds Espresso at 630 East Tudor Road near Old Seward Highway simply because it stayed open later than similar coffee stands. There were several other stands along Huffman Road that he considered, all of them comparable to the Common Grounds shop, but he had ultimately set his sights on the turquoise-blue colored stand with purple trim located in the parking lot of the Midtown Alaska Club fitness center. Like scores of other coffee shops in the city of Anchorage, the Common Grounds stand encompassed only about eight feet in width, and not much more in length. Typically only one employee manned the stand at a time, and most customers simply drove up to the window, placed their order, and soon continued on their way.

He had staked out the Common Grounds location a few days before, casually walking by to see how busy it tended to be at night. He had parked his white pick-up truck at the same Home Depot lot he was parked in again now. Then he had walked down Tudor Road, a busy, four-lane thoroughfare located near the University of Anchorage, until he passed by the coffee shop standing by itself at the edge of the Alaska Club parking lot. Wary about getting too close, he had made sure to keep at least 100 yards away, always staying by Tudor Road so that no one would notice him.

Now the irrepressible urge had taken root again, the irresistible craving once again controlled him. He was ready. It was time.

A light snow began to fall as he stepped out of his truck and started walking toward the Common Grounds stand. He did not have a specific plan in mind. He was going to at least rob the coffee shop, he knew that much for certain, but like many of his more recent outings, he was largely "playing it by ear." Since he did not know for sure how many people would be in the coffee shop, he was open to whatever the situation afforded him. However, kidnapping and murder were on his mind.

"The Common Grounds coffee stand where Samantha Koenig worked on Tudor Road in Anchorage, Alaska." (FBI Files)

Hands thrust deep in the pockets of his dark-colored coat, the shadowy figure walked through the IHOP parking lot, across Denali Street and down the sidewalk to the light at the corner of Tudor Road and Denali. He crossed Tudor and walked east, clutching a .22 Taurus handgun that he concealed in the pocket of his jacket. He had long since removed the battery from his cell phone, a practice he followed religiously any time he was on the hunt.

The snowfall intensified as he made his way across the parking lot of the Alaska Club and continued on to Common Grounds. There had been record levels of snowfall in recent days, and the berms formed from the accumulating powder were rising higher and higher. As he walked up to the coffee shop's order window, he could see an attractive young woman with long brown hair working inside. Her green shirt sleeves were rolled up as she arranged various items in the shop. She was alone, and it looked like she was getting ready to close for the night. But it was not coffee that he wanted. He was seeking a different kind of stimulant, another type of temporary high.

He calmly stepped to the window and ordered an Americano.

Eighteen-year-old Samantha Koenig had barely been able to contain her excitement when she landed the job as a barista at the Common Grounds Espresso coffee stand. The job perfectly suited the gregarious, brown-eyed brunette with the contagious laugh and infectious smile. Her welcoming personality and friendly demeanor had quickly made her a customer favorite at the stand, and although she had only been working there for a month, she had already developed a loyal following of regulars. Many said that within a few seconds of meeting her, they felt like they had a friend for life. Of course, her girl-next-door good looks helped win her repeat customers as well. Many drove well out of their way to spend a few minutes with the attractive young woman who always managed to brighten their day. For Samantha, it was not an act. She enjoyed getting to know new people and she genuinely cared about each and every customer who came to see her. She had that rarest of combinations: beauty both inside and out.

On that fateful Wednesday, Samantha's work shift had started out like any other day. Between preparing customers' orders, refilling supplies, and keeping things clean, she had stayed plenty busy. The time flew by as usual, and near the end of her shift, her cell phone rang. She smiled when she saw her father's phone number displayed. He was calling to check on her, something he did without fail every shift that she worked. She answered the phone and nearly sweet-talked her dad into bringing her dinner, but he was still at work and could not make it to the stand before she closed up for the night.

Although he could be an intimidating figure with his stocky build, long hair, and black leather biker's jacket, James Koenig had always had a soft spot for his daughter, and she, in turn, had always been a daddy's girl. The protective father in him had not wanted her to take the job at the coffee stand at all. Working in the stand, by herself, at night, just did not seem safe to him, but his initial resistance eventually caved in to her pleas. It always did. He could never deny her something that she really wanted. He was wrapped around her finger and they both knew it.

On this particular night, James had called his daughter from work during a quick break, and since he did not have much time to talk, they kept their conversation short.

"I'll see you at home later," he told her, and then as always, added, "Love you, honey" before hanging up.

"Okay," she said affectionately, "I love you too, Dad."

After hanging up, Samantha glanced at the clock and noticed that it was getting close to 7:00 p.m. She started straightening up around the shop in preparation for the last hour of her shift.

At 7:55 p.m., just before closing time, a man's voice addressed her from the ordering window.

"Could I get an Americano, please?"

Samantha was startled by the sudden sound of the man's voice. She had been so focused on cleaning up the store that she had not noticed him step up to the window, but it did not take long for her to regain her composure. After all, the man looked harmless enough.

"Sure, what size?" she asked, flashing him the same warm, friendly smile she gave all of her customers.

"Make it a large," he replied casually.

"Okay, it'll just be a sec," she said, still smiling.

Samantha turned around, grabbed an empty cup, and started

preparing his order. Thirty seconds later, she returned to the window and handed him his order.

"That'll be . . . " she stopped in mid-sentence, an involuntary gasp escaping her lips as the man pulled out a gun and pointed it at her.

"This is a robbery," he told her, his voice as calm as it had been when he ordered his Americano.

Her heart pounding with adrenaline, Samantha raised her hands above her head and backed away.

"Turn off the lights," he ordered.

Samantha complied without hesitation, too frightened to think about pressing the panic button located just inches from the light switch.

Six

As the coffee stand's lights went out, the drab figure at the window spotted someone sitting in a car at an automobile dealership across from the Alaska Club. The individual in the car was smoking a cigarette and watching him. Although the gunman could tell that the person sitting in the car was suspicious, he stayed calm. He would not abandon his plans because of a random onlooker. Instead, he kept talking to Samantha, casually, as if he was a regular customer or a boyfriend stopping by at the end of her shift. He told her to smile and nod like they were having a friendly conversation, all the while keeping the gun hidden in his sleeve. The ruse worked perfectly. After a few minutes, the anonymous watcher in the car ended his short surveillance, pulled out of the parking lot, and drove away.

No more witnesses in sight, the shady figure hoisted himself through the coffee stand's window. He told Samantha to get on her knees against the wall, and then he bound her hands behind her back with plastic cable ties.

"My dad's coming to pick me up soon," Samantha volunteered, hoping to scare her assailant away. "He'll be here any minute."

The intruder seemed unfazed by her words, so she tried again, adding whatever she could think of to try to talk him out of whatever he planned to do.

"They have surveillance cameras here, you know. If you rob this place, they'll figure out who you are. And the alarm will go off when I open the cash door. Besides, we really don't have much money here anyway."

Although he showed no reaction to her statements, Samantha's assailant was having second thoughts about what to do with her. He had not anticipated that she would not have a car parked nearby. If he went through with taking her, he would have to break two fundamental rules. The first rule of the hunt was never hunt near home. It was a rule he had always heeded well, until now. The second rule was to never use his own vehicle for abductions. Bringing his own vehicle into the equation would exponentially increase his risk of being caught, but something about Samantha compelled him to chance it. Her acquiescence to his demands during their initial encounter emboldened him. He savored the feeling of power. It gave him a rush of exhilaration unlike anything he had ever experienced before.

"I kind of lost self-control I guess you could say," he later told law enforcement. "I was feeling a little invincible. Against my judgment, I just kept going with it even though I had already told myself that if whoever was there didn't have a car, then I wasn't going to do anything more than rob them and tie them up."

Samantha's fear and absolute compliance had energized him. It made him want more.

"There was something about her, like the way she reacted, that made me want to just keep going with it," he explained. "I was just on a real adrenaline rush. I thought I could just walk her right down the street – and I had never done anything that brazen before, and I was determined at that point that it was going to happen regardless of what I had to do."

Having secured Samantha with zip ties, the opaque intruder peered out the coffee stand's window to make sure that no one was coming. In the parking lot near the stand, several people were walking to or from their cars, oblivious to what was happening inside. Confident that no Good Samaritans were on their way to try to save the day, he shut the stand's window, then locked and barred it.

"What's your name?" he asked calmly.

"Sam," she managed to reply despite her fear.

"Well, Sam, we're going to go for a little walk."

He grabbed some napkins off the countertop and pushed them into her mouth to gag her. Then, less than ten minutes after his arrival, he stepped out of the Common Grounds coffee shop with Samantha beside him. He guided her on his right, holding her close to him to make it appear that they were young lovers enjoying the warmth of each other's company on a cold winter's night. As they left the shop, he closed the door behind them, and Samantha wondered whether she would ever see it again.

Months later, investigators would ask him what his intentions were in abducting an employee from the coffee stand.

"Since you were going on a cruise the next day, what were you planning on doing with that person?"

After a brief pause, he cleared his throat and answered.

"Well, I wasn't going to bring her with me," he grinned.

Now, as they walked out of the coffee shop, Samantha's abductor put his arm around her, while steadying the gun just out of sight in his gloved hand.

"I'm going to be holding onto you," he told her. "I want you to act like you're my girlfriend and you've had too much to drink, so it looks like I'm just helping you walk, okay?"

"Okay," she murmured nervously in reply.

They started walking west down Tudor, retracing the path he had taken to reach the coffee stand. When they were about 200 feet from the stand, Samantha suddenly bolted from his grasp. She darted away from him for the first few steps, but then slowed, running clumsily, sloshing through patches of partially melted snow. He gave chase and quickly caught up to her, tackling her from behind. Pushing the gun against her ribs, he warned what would happen if she tried to get away again.

"I don't want to hurt you," he hissed, "but this gun is loaded with very quiet ammo that can kill you. Don't make me shoot you. Do you understand?"

She nodded to let him know that she took his warning seriously.

"We're just going to stand back up and pretend like we're best buddies, and I'm going to keep my arm around you."

He pressed the barrel of the gun into her ribs as they stood. He kept it there while they walked, as a reminder, but there was no need. The look of fear in her eyes clearly conveyed that she had received the message. She would not be causing any more problems.

When they reached the man's bone-white truck, several people were getting into a Suburban parked next to it, but he remained undeterred. He still had his insurance policy, the police scanner. He knew that if anyone called the police, he could easily "scrap the whole plan" and get away. Nobody would be able to identify him beyond a general description that could fit a large portion of the Anchorage population. He slowed his pace to allow the Suburban time to drive away, and then unlocked the front passenger door of his truck.

Samantha's hands were still tied behind her back, so he helped her climb inside the passenger's seat before closing the door behind her. After taking a quick glance around the parking lot, he walked to the driver's side of the truck, opened the door, and slid into the front seat. As he closed the door, he turned toward Samantha.

"Do you have a debit card?" he asked.

"Ye . . . yes," she stammered in reply. "I share one with my boyfriend, but I don't have it with me. It's in his truck."

The man glared at her, trying to gauge whether she was telling the truth.

"So where's his truck?"

"He parks it on the street in front of our house," she said. "He always parks at the same spot."

"What about a cell phone?"

"My phone's at the coffee stand," she answered softly, "but it's not working very well."

"All right, listen," he said as he put the passenger seatbelt around her. "This is what's going to happen. We're going to go for a drive and I'm going to hold you for ransom. I'll make a ransom demand to your family by phone a little later."

Samantha silently breathed a sigh of relief. She knew that her dad would give anything for her safe return.

"My family doesn't really have much money," she said, hoping that her abductor would decide to let her go.

"Don't worry, they'll get the money. I'll take care of it, but you need to do exactly what I say. Understand?"

Samantha nodded in reply.

"We're going to drive around for a while and you're going to keep your head turned toward me," he said. "Don't look out of the windows or try to signal anyone. If you do, I'll notice, and you won't like what will happen," he warned.

Just before 8:30 p.m., Samantha's abductor pulled his truck onto Denali Street and drove toward Northern Lights Boulevard, monitoring the police scanner for any signs of trouble or any mention of the Common Grounds coffee shop. Everything sounded normal.

While driving, he realized that his captive was not well restrained in the front seat. If she unbuckled her seat belt and opened the passenger door, she would be able to slip out before he could do anything to stop her. He needed to move her to the back seat so he could better secure her.

They stopped for a red light at the intersection of Denali and

Northern Lights. Two Anchorage Police Department patrol cars pulled up beside them. Samantha's heart raced as she thought about trying to signal the police, but then she remembered what happened the last time she had tried to get away. She sat paralyzed with indecision. Before she could gather the courage to do something, the light turned green and the patrol cars pulled away.

Her kidnapper turned left onto Northern Lights and headed to Lynn Ary Park. He pulled into a corner of the parking lot near the baseball fields and looked around. Two cars were parked in another part of the lot, and he could see several people with ski equipment walking toward them. He waited until they loaded their equipment and drove off, then he stepped out of his truck and opened the rear door.

He took out all of the tools in the backseat, wrapped them in a tarp in the bed of the pickup, and covered the seat with painter's drop cloths. Then he noticed that Samantha was shivering.

"Are you cold?" he asked.

"Yes," she said quietly, "a little."

Folding the truck's jump seat down, he fashioned a bed for her out of the drop cloths and some coats to help keep her warm. He put two cable ties around her wrists, pulling them tight like handcuffs, and ran several other ties between the two on her wrists to form a chain. Then he secured the chain to her seatbelt with some 36-inch-long cable ties that he wrapped around her. About twenty minutes had passed since he first pulled into the parking lot of the park.

Having situated Samantha more securely, he remembered that he needed a cell phone to send a ransom message to her family. Using his own phone was not an option. It would be way too risky. He thought about buying a prepaid phone at a nearby Walmart, and even drove from the park to the Walmart parking lot, but eventually concluded that it would be too much of a gamble. He might subsequently be spotted on the store's surveillance video. His hostage might also take the opportunity to scream for help or try to break out of the truck. Besides, the ransom text would be most believable if it came from Samantha's own phone. Since there was still no mention of Common Grounds on the police scanner, he felt comfortable returning to the coffee shop to retrieve the phone.

Having made the decision to return to the coffee shop, he edged his truck out of the Walmart parking lot and drove back to Tudor before pulling off at the Alaska Club and parking in the back. He thought that his captive might try to get away again, so he reminded her that he still had his police scanner.

———————

Around the time that Samantha's abductor left Walmart to retrieve her cell phone from Common Grounds, her boyfriend, Duane Tortolani, stopped by the coffee stand looking for her. Growing increasingly worried about her, Tortolani repeatedly texted and called Samantha as her phone chimed unseen in the dark, empty shop. Receiving no answer or reply, he pulled up to the stand's order window and peered inside, wondering where she could be.

———————

Samantha's captor opened the door of his truck and stepped out into the snow, leaving her covered up with drop cloths. Eyes and ears alert for anything unusual, he walked around the side of the Alaska Club and headed toward the Common Grounds coffee stand.

Seven

Everything was quiet as an indistinct, darkly dressed man approached the Common Grounds coffee shop. The parking lot that had been filled with cars and pedestrians hours earlier was now nearly deserted. Even Duane Tortolani had departed by the time Samantha's abductor returned to the coffee stand. He opened the stand's door, still unlocked, and had no problem locating Samantha's cell phone and car keys. On the floor by the window, he noticed a couple of plastic pieces cut from the ends of the zip ties that he had used to bind her. He grabbed them and arranged things in the shop to make it look like Samantha had closed up like normal. Her cell phone started ringing as he began to leave. Without answering, he glanced at the caller display and noticed that it was now nearly 11:00 p.m.

Having retrieved the cell phone, he returned to his truck and found Samantha exactly the way he had left her.

"Good girl," he said with a smile.

He slid into the driver's seat and sent a short text to her boyfriend. Pretending to be Samantha, he typed that she was mad and would not be home that night because she needed some time alone. After sending the text, he pulled the battery out of the cell phone to make it harder to track.

He started the truck's engine and pulled out of the parking lot. Before long, he heard a faint voice from the back seat.

"Mister, I don't mean to bother you," Samantha said softly, "but I really need to pee."

A mix of anger and annoyance flashed across his face.

"All right," he sighed, "I'll find someplace for you to go."

He unwrapped a cigar as he drove. After lighting it, he took a puff and glanced back at her.

"You want to share this?" he asked.

"Uh…sure," she said hesitantly, not quite sure how to respond.

He handed the cigar to her and she slowly sucked in a mouthful of smoke.

"Thanks," she said, handing it back to him.

"Did you go to school around here?" she asked, hoping that engaging him in conversation would make him less likely to hurt her.

"Shut up," he replied curtly. He knew what she was trying to do. They drove for a while in silence. Then she decided to try again.

"Where'd you get these cigars?" she asked. "They're really good."

"I said to shut up," he hissed, the harsher tone of his voice clearly meant to convey a warning.

This time she stayed quiet for good. The man drove to Earthquake Park and stopped.

"You can pee here," he told her.

He walked with her to the woods and let her relieve herself, but waited a few minutes before returning to the truck because he spotted a car coming toward them. He watched the car as it came closer, but then it slowed down, turned around, and drove away. When the way was clear, he took Samantha back to the truck.

As he started the engine, the truck's low fuel warning light came on. He glared at the light, muttered something to himself, and started looking for the closest gas station. He spotted a Tesoro station a couple of miles down the road and pulled into the parking lot. Quickly, but as inconspicuously as possible, he pumped a few gallons of gas and then decided to head home.

He eventually turned onto Spurr Lane, a quiet, unassuming street of well-kept homes on a cul-de-sac in the Turnagain neighborhood of West Anchorage. As he approached the modest house that he shared with his girlfriend, the headlights of his truck illuminated a yellow-orange street sign warning of a "DEAD END." He backed into the driveway at 2456 Spurr Lane, and parked close to a storage shed beside the house. He turned around and looked Samantha in the eye.

"Sit tight for a little while," he instructed her. "I have to do some things to the truck. Just stay still and be quiet and I'll be back in a minute."

Samantha could hear clanging and scraping noises as he put a metal tool rack and box on the truck. She guessed that he was trying to disguise it. When he finished attaching the parts, he stood next to the truck trying to figure out how to get Samantha into the shed without anyone seeing her. It would be an inherently risky endeavor. In the short span of time that had passed since he had parked the truck, several neighbors had already passed by the front of the driveway walking their dogs. On top of that, his girlfriend was still awake inside the house. After debating with himself for several minutes, he decided that he had to chance it. He blindfolded Samantha, and after taking one last look around, led her from the truck into the shed.

He had prepared the shed for a potential guest before leaving the house earlier in the evening. Two heaters were running, keeping the inside of the shed warm, and a 9 x 12 foot tarp covered most of the floor. To immobilize his captive, he grabbed a piece of rope and noosed it around her neck, then fastened it to the walls with several screws. He untied Samantha's hands, which were still bound behind her back, and then tied them up in front of her so that she could smoke or use a five-gallon bucket as a toilet.

"I've got some errands to do around town to get the ransom thing going," he told her. "So I'm going to leave you here for a while, but I've still got my scanner with me. If I hear anything about reports of screaming or any disturbance from you, I'll be back here before the cops can come. And I won't be happy," he warned.

The fear in her eyes told him that she would stay quiet. But as an added precaution, he turned on a radio and raised the volume so that music blared loudly inside the shed. If Samantha tried screaming for help, the music would drown out her pleas. He asked her for her home address, went inside the house, pulled the address up on Mapquest, and printed the resulting map and directions. Then he took the map back to the shed and had her point out exactly where her boyfriend's truck would be parked. Satisfied that he could find it, he climbed into his girlfriend's silver Nissan Xterra SUV and drove away, leaving Samantha bound and alone in the dark.

———————————

Shortly after 2:30 in the morning, he approached the address Samantha had given him. He pulled over about three blocks away, then walked the rest of the way. Dressed entirely in black, he easily blended into the darkness that enveloped the street. Samantha's boyfriend's truck was parked in front of her house exactly where she said it would be. After using her key to unlock the driver's side door, he found her wallet tucked behind the passenger side visor. Flipping open the wallet, he grabbed Samantha's driver's license and a Credit Union 1 VISA debit card, but as he stepped back out of the truck, he heard the unmistakable sound of a house door creaking open.

Looking toward the house, he saw a shadowy figure in the doorway. The figure took a few steps toward him, and then abruptly stopped. After a few seconds, a male voice addressed him.

"Can I help you with something?" the voice said guardedly.

He stared back at the dark figure, silently readying his knife. Suddenly, the figure in the doorway darted back into the house.

Seizing the opportunity to get away, he ran down the street and ducked behind a snow bank. After catching his breath, he peeked around the mound of snow to see if anyone was following him. The street was deserted save for a few parked cars frosted with fresh snow. With no pursuer in sight, he hurried back to his girlfriend's car and sped off. Now he had everything he needed.

Invigorated by what he planned to do next, he returned home. He poured a glass of wine and tiptoed into the bedroom where his girl-friend lay sleeping. He took a purple handkerchief out of a dresser drawer and went back downstairs. After putting on a head lamp, he returned to the shed.

When he opened the shed door, Samantha was still sitting on the five-gallon bucket that he had left for her. A foam mat and fleece sleeping bag were still spread out underneath the bucket. She did not appear to have tried to get away. He was not surprised. Fear had a way of subduing the mind. Besides, he had made her believe that she would soon be released in exchange for ransom money, so she had an incentive to cooperate.

The shed was dark except for the beam of light coming from his head lamp. Samantha squinted at him.

"Is everything working out okay?" she asked hopefully. "Were you able to get a hold of my dad for the ransom?"

"Yeah, it's all fine," he assured her.

He unscrewed the rope from the wall, careful to keep the ties on her wrists secured and the noose around her neck.

"Lay down on the mat on your stomach," he said sternly.

He watched as she complied, then he ran two pieces of rope through the cable ties on her hands. After tying knots in the ends of the rope, he screwed it to the wall nearly level with the ground, so that her arms were pressed against the floor and stretched slightly behind her head. Then he pinned her legs down as well. He could feel her trembling in terror.

"Please don't rape me," she pleaded.

He moved his head closer to her, so close that she could feel the warmth of his breath on her ear.

"You knew this was coming," he whispered as tears began trickling down her cheeks.

He tied a six-foot piece of nylon rope around her ankles and secured it with a knot. He knew she would try to scream eventually so he gagged her with the purple handkerchief by winding it up and tying it around her head. Then he grabbed a 36-inch cable tie and put it around her neck, not so tight as to choke her, but tight enough that she could feel it constricting her.

"All I have to do is pull this," he warned, gripping the cable tie like a noose, "and once I pull it, there's no going back."

She nodded that she understood. Aroused by the feeling of having absolute control over her, he pulled out a black folding knife with a three-inch blade and started cutting off her clothes. First, the back of her tee-shirt and bra, and then both of her black, spandex pant legs. Her thong underwear was the last piece of clothing to go. As each piece of clothing came off, he stuffed it into a black trash bag. He did the same with each cable tie that he cut. Her purse and wallet were already in the bag.

Samantha shuddered as he applied KY jelly between her legs. Although she was gagged, he could still hear her crying. He stood up so that he could admire his handiwork. It excited him to see her suffering. He took off his clothes and put on a condom. Then he mounted her from behind, forcing himself inside of her.

Several songs came and went on the radio as he slid in and out of her, but just as he was about to finish, he stopped and pulled all the way out. Samantha sobbed silently, devastated by what she had endured, but finding some measure of relief in the fact that it was over.

Her reprieve did not last long. She felt a sudden piercing sensation and winced in pain as he penetrated her anally. She started to scream, but he pulled the cable tie around her neck tighter and told her to shut up. After several minutes of agony, he finished and slid away from her.

"Are you going to kill me?" she whimpered, her voice trailing off with lost hope.

His silence spoke volumes. Her heart pounded as her mind raced a million directions at once trying to decide what to do, desperate to satisfy him in order to stay alive.

"You know, I give really good blow jobs," she said, struggling to keep from breaking down in despair.

"That sounds like a good way to get my dick bit off," he replied with a cold smirk.

Samantha giggled nervously, her despondent laugh betraying an utter loss of hope. The man relished the intoxicating sensation of her fear.

Without warning, he yanked the cable tie as hard as he could, closing it tightly around her neck. He continued pulling on it as he straddled her, using such force that her head and chest lifted up off the floor. Samantha never made a sound as the life slowly drained from her, as he silently strangled her in the darkness.

When she had been still for several minutes, he grabbed another nylon rope and tied it to the cable tie around her neck. Then he used the rope to hang her from a nearby shelf, keeping the front of her body elevated off the floor to maintain pressure on her neck. Satisfied that she was sufficiently positioned, he finished his glass of wine, put on his pants, and went back into the house to shower.

Next came his normal household duties. He woke up his daughter, fed the dogs, and made sure that all of his bags were packed. About fifteen minutes later, he went back to the shed and untied the rope. He pulled Samantha's lifeless body onto the foam mattress and wrapped the tarp around her. He opened the lower cabinets in the shed as far as they would go, shoved her inside, and shut the cabinet door, careful to conceal her body so that if anyone opened the cabinet door they would just see a tarp being stored inside.

After leaving the shed, he double-locked its doors, went back into the house, and called a cab for a ride to the airport. He had a flight to catch to Houston, Texas, where he would make his way to New Orleans for a cruise that he had booked months earlier. The cruise provided a convenient reason for leaving town.

As the plane took off, Samantha's killer smiled to himself, certain that his planning and precautions had paid off, and still savoring the post-killing high that drove him to do it again and again. Confident that the twenty-degree weather would preserve Samantha's body until he returned from his trip, he settled into his seat and finished a quick drink. Gazing out the window at the cold city below, he smiled to himself at the thought of all the people who would soon be trying to find her. Then he tilted his chair back, closed his eyes, and fell into a deep, pleasant sleep.

Eight

M ichelle Robbins, owner of the Common Grounds shop where Samantha had worked, was not worried about her initially. She had seen her coffee stand girls have bad nights in which they did not follow proper closing procedures. Perhaps it was Samantha's turn to have an off night.

Robbins and her husband had opened up the stand on Tudor Road nearly a decade earlier, and its success had spawned an expansion to three locations around the Anchorage area. The worst thing that had happened in all of those years of operation involved only property damage. During the predawn hours in January 2009, a drunk driver being pursued by the police had gone off the road, rolled over and over across the parking lot, and smashed into the Common Grounds stand located at Old Seward Road. The store's surveillance camera captured the image of the vehicle crashing through the wall and obliterating much of the store's interior. Fortunately, the coffee stand had been closed at the time and no one was inside when the accident occurred. Now, two years later, Common Grounds security cameras would again play an important role, but this time with much more at stake than the loss of coffee supplies.

After receiving a telephone call from Samantha's worried father,

Robbins and her husband went on the internet to view the prior night's video from the coffee stand's security camera. It soon became apparent that Samantha had not abandoned her job site or simply forgotten to clean up. The security video showed a frightened looking girl apparently responding to instructions from an obscure figure at the ordering window. The dark figure's boldness was underscored by the fact that a bystander could be seen in the video sitting in a pick-up truck no more than fifty feet from the coffee stand, yet that person never seemed to notice anything wrong.

"They were just oblivious," Robbins's husband said.

He called the Anchorage Police Department shortly after 12:30 in the afternoon to report what he had seen on the security video. He brushed off any suggestions of insufficient safety measures at the coffee stand, pointing to its multiple surveillance cameras and built-in alarm with a panic button.

"We took it seriously," he said. "We have young women working in here."

He described Samantha as very energetic with a bubbly personality, someone who had a natural ability to put others at ease.

"She had already built a loyal customer base," Robbins pointed out.

Melanie Ornelas, who worked the morning shift at the coffee stand, had found cold cups of coffee sitting out on the counter when she arrived to open for the day. Samantha's belongings had been left in her cubby box as well, along with a note asking if she needed to work on Saturday.

"It looked like, in the middle of making a drink, she just left," Ornelas said.

She had felt safe working at the coffee stand before, but no longer.

"It's weird. I mean, it could happen to anyone," she said. "Everyone, I think, is like, 'Oh, that could never happen to me.' But it very well could happen to anyone."

At the House of Harley, where Samantha had worked in sales during the summer and fall of 2011 just before taking the job at Common Grounds, former co-workers remembered her as a tomboy who loved the Pittsburgh Steelers and her pit-bull mix that her father had given her as a present. Although she had a lot of friends and made new ones easily, she seemed to be a homebody who liked to stay close to home.

"I think her dad was real protective of her," Heather Cartwright recalled. "I think her friends usually ended up at her house."

She described Samantha as a "beautiful girl who didn't really know that she was beautiful" and who struggled with the usual insecurities of a teenaged girl. Cartwright was sure of one thing: Samantha had not disappeared voluntarily.

"She wouldn't let her dad anguish like this on purpose," she said.

Samantha's boyfriend, Duane Tortolani, had a hard time understanding Sam's disappearance.

"She's a really good person and this shouldn't be happening to her. She doesn't deserve this."

Pam Koenig Garner, Samantha's aunt, echoed the feeling.

"We're missing a wonderful, great girl that needs to come home to us," she said.

Tortolani had met Samantha because they attended the same high school, and after she friended him on Facebook, they started talking online and then eventually in person. About three months later, she invited him to her house for a BBQ with her dad. Tortolani had been attracted to her physically, but he also found her amicable personality appealing.

"Sam was a good person," Tortolani recalled. "She had a good heart."

He liked how she was always kind to whoever she came into contact with, and she had a great sense of humor. He and Samantha played video games, hung out at the mall together, and just enjoyed each other's company at home.

About ten months before her abduction, Tortolani had moved into the house that Sam shared with her dad. Tortolani had been kicked out of his house for drinking, and Sam had given her dad an "ultimatum" that she would not come home unless Tortolani could stay there. After seeing that she was serious, James Koenig grudgingly allowed Tortolani to move in, but with certain conditions attached, including that he do chores around the house to help out. The first month after the move-in had been awkward, but James eventually warmed up to Tortolani and became like a second father to him.

Now Tortolani was haunted by the last time he saw Samantha. Since he had a passion for cooking, he took a job as a chef at Suite 100, a fine-dining steak house at Old Seward and Diamond, less than two miles from the Common Grounds coffee stand where Samantha worked near the intersection of Tudor and Old Seward.

"Sam loved my cooking," he said.

On the afternoon of January 31, he started walking to work since his truck had recently been t-boned in a parking lot accident. He stopped by Common Grounds on the way so he could, see Samantha, and she asked how he was getting to work.

"I'm walking," he told her.

"You're crazy," she exclaimed. "It's too cold. Take my truck."

"Then how will you get home?"

"My cousin Dan can pick me up," she said.

After further prodding, Tortolani reluctantly took her truck, but he secretly planned on coming back to get her after her shift ended at 8:00 p.m. because he did not trust her cousin to get her. He knew from experience that Dan drank too much to be reliable.

At 7:45 p.m., Tortolani asked his supervisor if he could leave for a little while so he could go pick up Sam and then come back to work. His boss gave him permission to leave on the condition that he first finished cleaning up the kitchen. By the time he made it to Common Grounds, it was nearly a quarter after 8.

As he approached the coffee stand, he noticed that the lights were off. This struck him as odd because Sam had always left them on after closing. He peered into the window, but she was nowhere to be found. He called her cell phone over and over, and texted her at least ten times, but received no answer or reply.

Alarmed by the strange circumstances, he called James Koenig to let him know that Sam was not there, but he had to get back to work. James told him not to worry too much about it. He figured that she would show up at home sooner or later. Still not wholly reassured, but willing to accept James's explanation for the moment, Tortolani drove back to the Suite 100 restaurant.

After getting off work at 11:30 p.m., Tortolani rushed home to find that Samantha still had not returned. James thought that she was probably in a bad mood about something and just needed time to vent. The suggestion did little to calm Tortolani's nerves. After a while, James went to bed, but Tortolani was too worried to sleep.

Several hours later, his cell phone sounded an incoming text. It was from Samantha's number. "I'm going to my friend's house for a few days, the text read. Tell my dad I love him. You won't hear from me until I come home."

Now he was sure something was wrong. He knew Sam and he knew that she would never ask him to relay a message to James through a text. She would call her dad herself.

Sometime between 3 and 4:00 in the morning, he heard a car door close outside the house. He sprang up from the sofa, hoping it was Sam. When he went out on the front porch to see if it was her, he saw a dark figure standing by his truck. The figure was clad all in black: black ski mask, black shirt, black pants, and black boots. He was leaning over, rummaging through the driver's side of the truck. Then the figure stopped, stepped out of the truck, and stared at Tortolani.

As the adrenaline surged through his veins, Tortolani dashed back into the house to get James, but by the time they returned to the porch, the dark figure was gone. They ran into the street and looked both directions, but there was not a soul in sight.

The days that followed were a blur of trying to find Samantha and being questioned by the police. At one point, it seemed like the APD suspected him of abducting her. All the while, he never stopped searching for Samantha, and never gave up hope that she was still alive.

James Koenig had not slept more than five hours over the past five days since Samantha's abduction. He kept thinking about how he had never wanted his daughter to work at the coffee shop in the first place. He had tried to talk her out of taking the job, but she had her heart on working there and wanted the tips for gas money. He had reluctantly given her his consent, but his concerns about her working at the coffee stand alone at night remained. It just did not seem safe.

And now his worst nightmare had come true.

"If I had my way, I'd do away with all of those coffee shops on the roadsides," he said adamantly.

He feared for his daughter's future.

"She has goals," he said emphatically. "She's got a good head and she's a smart kid."

Despite trying to keep a positive mindset, he could not stop himself from periodically thinking the worst. Now he was racking his brain trying to decide where to start searching for his missing girl.

"I'm hitting every place I can possibly think of to get any tip or inclination," he said with growing desperation.

On February 3, Anchorage police publicly announced that they now believed that Samantha had been abducted at gunpoint from the Common Grounds coffee shop. The police described her abductor as wearing a dark-colored, hooded sweatshirt and being significantly taller than the 5-feet 5-inch Koenig. They had initially treated Samantha's disappearance as a "suspicious" missing person case, but now officially deemed it to be an abduction.

Heavy snow fell from the sky as APD spokesman Dave Parker spoke to reporters near the coffee stand, bringing them up to date on the status of his department's investigative efforts. Since Samantha's abduction, more than a foot of snow had fallen, potentially concealing evidence at the crime scene and making the difficult task of finding her even more challenging. Parker stressed that no less than two dozen detectives were working the case, along with regular patrol officers and officers from the APD's Special Assignments and Vice Units. Although they had conducted countless interviews, pursued numerous leads, and reviewed hours of surveillance footage from area businesses, they had not come anywhere close to identifying a suspect.

"Anyone could be a suspect at this point," Detective Sladomir Markiewicz acknowledged.

On the other end of the parking lot, James Koenig passed out boxes of missing person flyers bearing a photo and description of his daughter, along with rolls of tape so that volunteers could put them up throughout Anchorage, Eagle River, Palmer, and Wasilla. Stating "KIDNAPPED" in bold letters across the top, the 7,000 flyers had been donated by Kinko's and the University of Alaska.

A third-generation Alaskan whose maternal grandmother had arrived in Dillingham nearly a century before, James Koenig grew up in a blue collar family in Anchorage. His father had been a plumber, his mother a municipal bus driver. After high school, James worked in the air and ground freight industry for twenty years, working his way up to operations manager. When persistent back problems forced him to find different work, he discovered that he had a talent for cooking and landed a job as a cook at The Indian House restaurant about fifteen minutes outside of Anchorage.

A tireless worker, he logged 15-hour days at the restaurant at least five days a week, and often six or seven. Then he met the woman who would become Samantha's mother, a fellow restaurant worker named Darlene. They quickly hit it off and dated a little over a year before getting married. Samantha Tesla Koenig – named in part after the hard rock band, Tesla – was born on August 30, 1993, several months before the wedding. They enjoyed a happy marriage for the first few years of Samantha's life, but the happiness waned over time and they eventually broke apart. Following their divorce, James was awarded sole custody of Samantha. He raised her as a single parent for the rest of her life.

Father and daughter enjoyed a particularly close relationship from the start, and Samantha quickly stole his heart. James was so protective of her, and so worried about Sudden Infant Death Syndrome, that he slept right beside Samantha's bassinet on a couch for the first six months of her life. Like any parent and child, they had their share of ups and downs, but as Samantha grew older, she became more than a daughter to James. She also became his best friend. No doubt due to the close relationship she enjoyed with her father, Sam developed into something of a tomboy.

"She was not by any means a girly-girl," James recalled fondly.

Sam liked camping, shooting, four-wheeling, and fishing with her father just as much as staying in and watching her favorite Will Farrell movies. She had started shooting a .22 rifle with James when she was just five years old. In addition to her tomboy pursuits, Sam enjoyed music and writing. In addition to writing songs and poetry, she played the clarinet in her high school band for two years. She also developed a passion for animals, a passion kindled early on when her father surprised her with a puppy that he had found for her on Craigslist. When James picked her up at junior high school that day, she immediately knew that he was up to something because she could see something rustling around in his coat. With her father grinning from ear to ear, she unzipped his coat and squealed with delight upon finding the furry, four-legged surprise. She named the dog Sheba, and the two quickly became inseparable. Before long, Sam decided that she wanted to be a veterinarian and she went to work amassing a collection of critters at the house.

As James put it, Sam "would have had a farm if I'd let her."

James had always admired his daughter's wit and genuineness. She was fun-loving and often sarcastic, but always truthful. She enjoyed being a "goofball" to put smiles on people's faces, and her laugh was "infectious." One of her favorite songs, "What You Give," was by the group that gave rise to her middle name. The song's message about living the life you choose so resonated with her that she resolved to pattern her life after it.

Now, on this cold February morning, James appealed to his daughter's abductor.

"I want to ask my daughter's captors to please send her home," he stated to an assembled group of reporters. Then he addressed the unknown abductor directly.

"I will give you anything in this world. I will meet you, I will give you whatever you want. Just please bring my daughter back."

He announced a $12,500 reward for information leading to Samantha's safe return.

"I don't know if my daughter's being fed, taken care of, if she's still alive, if she's getting any sleep," he said. "I don't think any of us are," he added, gesturing to a group of about forty friends and family members gathered in the parking lot around him. He handed out green-colored ribbons – Samantha's favorite color – and more of the "KID-NAPPED" posters, holding back tears as he did so.

"I couldn't get through this without you guys," he told the group of supporters, his voice slightly cracking. "I just need her home. Every day she's gone, the odds are against us."

In the midst of working on the latest legal crisis to come across his desk, Anchorage attorney Rex Butler received a phone call from Tammie Counts, the mother of Christopher Bird, an aspiring rap artist who had known Samantha Koenig. Counts's angry desperation came across clearly through the speaker phone as she described how her son, who used the stage name, Whyte Tyson, was being harassed by members of the community who believed that he was responsible for Samantha's kidnapping. Bird lived with his mother and they had been receiving harassing calls and even death threats since shortly after Samantha's disappearance. Bird became the object of such hostility because word had spread that Samantha sought a restraining order against him several months earlier, in November 2011. In seeking the order, Sam had asserted a "fear of death or personal injury" from Bird, who she alleged had sexually assaulted her in his home.

Chris had met Samantha in May through her "street brother," Mike Peterson, and she started coming over to the house to hang out. Tammie Counts had only complimentary things to say about her, describing Samantha as being very respectful and "very beautiful."

"She had a heart of gold," Counts said. "She was a very sweet girl."

Chris echoed his mom's recollection.

"Everybody loved her," he said, referring to Samantha. "There was not a bad bone in her body at all. She was really an awesome person."

According to Counts, Samantha and Chris engaged in consensual sex about six months after they met, but Sam later regretted it either because she felt guilty or because she worried that her boyfriend would find out. She sought the restraining order against Chris alleging that he assaulted her because she did not want her boyfriend to know what had really happened. That, combined with the fact that Chris had a similar body type as Samantha's kidnapper – tall, lean, and lanky – had quickly raised suspicions against him following her disappearance.

A couple of days after Samantha went missing, APD detectives showed up at Counts's house and asked Chris to come down to the station for questioning. They suspected that he had abducted Samantha out of anger and in retaliation for her allegations of sexual assault. Counts assured the police that Chris was at home, grounded, on the night of Samantha's abduction. But in the court of public opinion, he was already guilty. The community was convinced that Chris had taken her. Amidst the resulting wave of ill will and accusations, Chris was kicked out of barber school – losing the $6,000 he had paid into it in the process – because the owner did not want to have to deal with the backlash of having him there.

Chris had grown up as a bull rider and cowboy in North Carolina, but after falling in with the wrong crowd, he moved to Anchorage to get his life back on the right track. Now he was mixed up in another mess, one that took on a life of its own as the hostility against him from a large segment of the community continued to grow. Incited by what podcast host Chelsea Hoffman called a "lynch mob led by James Koenig," the situation grew so bad that Tammie Counts became too afraid to even go to the grocery store. She feared for her safety as well as the safety of her son and other children.

"I was scared to death," she said, describing the effect of the hostility directed at her family.

On February 7, in response to mounting public criticism for refusing to release the Common Grounds surveillance video showing Samantha's abduction, Lt. Michelle Bucher of the APD conveyed the rationale for the department's decision.

"Believe me, I understand how concerned her family is. How concerned the public is about this," Buchner explained. "But we also have to be concerned about the integrity of the investigation. If we felt that we could gain more, in terms of getting Samantha back right now, then we would be releasing it. We would have released it by now."

Lt. Dave Parker commented about what police had concluded from viewing the security video.

"You can clearly see that she is being taken against her will," he said, describing Samantha's reaction. "We know they left the area on foot. Did he have a car parked somewhere? Did he go to a friend's house? Investigators are absolutely beating the boards in the investigation and they are working very hard."

Parker reiterated a call for patience to allow the investigative process to play out.

"This is not a one-hour, TV cop drama," he said. "This is real life. And it takes time to work through these things."

The fact remained that, despite all of the hours APD investigators had spent working on the case, they were no closer to finding Samantha than they were the day she disappeared. And they still had no idea about the identity of the man who abducted her.

(Tammie & Iz - Tacoma, WA December 7, 2000)

Bored and in need of a job, Tammie Hawkins is scanning the want ads section of the Tacoma News Tribune when she notices a local chat line being advertised. On a whim, she dials the number and follows the prompts to listen to the personal ads that had been placed in her area.

One message in particular attracts her attention. It is from a 21-year-old man looking for a white female between the ages of 18 and 25 in the Colville, Washington, area. Being that Tammie is one-half Native American and one-half African American, 30-years old, and living in Tacoma, she does not even vaguely match the man's criteria. None-theless, she feels compelled to contact him to let him know that there is a problem with his message. He had evidently tried to leave a voice reply to another woman who had responded to his ad, but in doing so he had recorded over his original greeting for the ad. While Tammie finds it screamingly funny, she also feels a little sorry for the guy. Still giggling to herself, she leaves a message to alert him about the problem.

Tammie was born in Oakland, California, in 1969 to an African-American father and a Native American mother who traced her Makah Indian ancestors back hundreds of years in Neah Bay, a tiny village of less than 900 people on the Makah Reservation in Clallam County in the northwest corner of Washington. An indigenous people whose ancestors first inhabited the area more than 3,800 years ago, the Makah Indian Tribe referred to themselves as Kwih-dich-chuh-ahtx, "the people who live by the rocks and seagulls." Skilled mariners for centuries, the Tribe's primary industry revolved around fishing. Over half of the reservation's residents were unemployed and many lived below the poverty line, including Tammie's mom, who was only 19 years old when she had Tammie, the pregnancy the end result of her naivety when she became involved with an older man, an African-American sailor in the Navy.

Tammie's parents married when she was three years old, but separated within a year or two, and subsequently divorced. Her father, who had been raised in an orphanage until he was nine, was gone much of the time, and it was an open secret that he had another girlfriend, even while Tammie's mother was pregnant with her two younger sisters.

As a half-black Indian, Tammie was the target of racial slurs on the Makah reservation throughout her childhood, and due to her mother's alcoholism, Tammie had been in and out of foster care multiple times by her tenth birthday. Tammie and her sisters grew up in poverty surrounded by alcohol and drug abuse. They lived in run- down, dilapidated houses and trailers with no plumbing or electricity, and Tammie was sexually abused – something which "runs rampant on reservations" – on numerous occasions. When she was ten years old, she watched as her mom was beaten and raped.

Tammie grew up as a tomboy, playing kick-ball and basketball, and having dirt-bomb fights at the local creek. Due to her family situation, she always felt that she was worth less than others and that she had to work twice as hard as everyone else. A "huge overachiever," she played on her high school's basketball team, served as editor for the yearbook, and was elected to student council. Her grades always started out as A's and B's, but by the end of the year inevitably dropped to C's because she could never manage to stay focused.

After babysitting for families on the reservation for a few years, she started working in the tribe's summer employment program when she was thirteen. The legacy of her mother's alcoholism reared its ugly head when Tammie was sixteen. Her drinking quickly spiraled out of control, and a month before she turned seventeen, she joined Alcoholics Anonymous.

————

Tammie has lived in a duplex in University Place in Tacoma since moving there from the Makah Indian Reservation. She has done well

working as a service adviser for a Ford dealership for several years,
but she recently lost her job due to a disagreement with a customer.
Now she is unemployed and contacting a total stranger about a
personal ad that he placed. And she is surprised when he quickly
replies back.

Nine

Detective Monique Doll, a tall, third-generation cop with long blonde hair, had just been assigned to the Anchorage Police Department's homicide squad a day earlier when she learned about Samantha Koenig's disappearance. Now, just her second day on the job, Doll faced the daunting task of trying to find Samantha.

A Home Depot parking lot security video provided Doll and her fellow detectives their best lead. The video, recorded from a camera hundreds of feet away, showed Koenig and her anonymous abductor walking to a white pick-up truck in the snow-covered parking lot. However, to their dismay, APD investigators discovered that 3,000 vehicles in the Anchorage area fit the profile of the truck. Over the next six weeks, they would scour the city tracking down virtually every one of those trucks.

Elsewhere in Anchorage, attorney Rex Butler assured the media that his client, Christopher Bird, had been at home the night that Samantha disappeared.

"The world's going to have to beat on someone else," he said dramatically, with obvious sarcasm.

———

The next day, coffee baristas from all around Anchorage held a candle-lighting ceremony at Sunrise Bagel & Espresso to honor Samantha. An Alaska State Trooper spoke to the group and gave tips to the young women about how to prevent and fend off attacks like the one experienced by Samantha.

———

By February 10, a donated motor home parked near the Common Grounds coffee stand served as the 24-hour operations base for James Koenig and his supporters in their efforts to find Samantha. Despite having hardly slept since his daughter's disappearance, Koenig manned the trailer non-stop, coordinating searches and spearheading distribution of the posters that now approached 45,000 in number. Operating on one or two hours of sleep a night, he would live in the motor home for nearly a month, fielding over 10,000 phone calls from tipsters during that time. Like George Murtie in the Currier case, he chased down every lead that came in, often hanging up the phone and racing across town to check out a potentially helpful tip. Every tip raised his hopes with the possibility of his daughter's safe return, but every one led to the disappointment of a dead end.

"It all kind of meshed together after a while," he said, recalling how the sheer volume of tips had "frazzled my brain."

Throughout it all, he continued to be overwhelmed by the support from members of the community, people who, until recently, he had never met and who had themselves never met Samantha.

"I never expected people to drop their lives like this, he explained.

"They are the true heroes. Most of them I don't even know, but they're treating Samantha as one of their own."

Perhaps part of the reason for the community's outpouring of support could be traced to the fact that, by taking Samantha from one of the popular coffee stands dotting the Anchorage area, the abductor had struck at one of the hallmarks of the city, something the citizens of Anchorage considered fundamental to their way of life. As *Alaska Daily News* columnist Julia O'Malley pointed out, Anchorage boasted the highest number of coffee stands per capita in the country. Such stands stood as a "signature Anchorage phenomena" staffed with attractive young women, young women who now felt increasingly unsafe.

Ashton Stoltzfus-Avis, a barista at the Hot Spot coffee shop, expressed a reaction shared among many of the young women working the city's coffee stands.

"As a fellow barista, it's always been at the back of my mind, she said, but for it to actually happen, and happen so out of the blue, I mean, it's scary for anybody. Even not as a barista, just as a young lady."

Sari Phillips, a barista at the Kodiak Kup, spoke of a similar feeling of shock and unease.

"I know a lot of girls that work in coffee shops are scared. My family got me pepper spray. I know a lot of girls' families are doing that."

Another barista, Christina Johnson from Qwik Cup Espresso, summarized the general sentiment.

"This shouldn't happen, especially in our small little town, at the coffee shop around the corner," she said.

On February 11, the same day that Samantha's killer was returning to New Orleans following a cruise, Samantha's family and friends were joined by approximately 1,000 supporters from the Anchorage community for a candlelight vigil in Town Square Park in downtown Anchorage. James Koenig was nearly overcome with emotion as a procession of well-wishers approached him to offer him words of encouragement.

"It's powerful," he said as they continued to pack into the square. "I don't think there's words to really describe it. It's amazing how a community can come together."

Then, turning towards the center of the park, he addressed the growing crowd.

"I just don't know how to thank you all. You're my heroes. I never expected it to turn out like this. That's why I love living in Alaska."

City Church Pastor Richard Irwin also addressed the crowd, calling on them to comfort and support one another. Before offering a prayer, he appealed to Samantha's unidentified abductor.

"I have an idea that you are probably listening right now," he said. "There is hope for you. But please, we are begging you, let Samantha go."

Soon hundreds of green and white balloons filled the air, released by many of those in the assembled crowd, along with floating lanterns. It was a touching moment of support and unity for a community in need of reassurance of its security. Kirsten Bowers, who had driven from Eagle River to attend the vigil, expressed the common feeling in the community.

"This guy has not only taken Samantha, he's taken our innocence," said Bowers, an Alaskan resident for nearly forty years. "It's just so random and so, I don't know, so not Alaska. Everybody's looking over their shoulders now. The innocence is lost. I don't know if we can ever regain that."

Christopher Bird knew that he would not be welcome at the vigil, so he and his brother watched it from a nearby apartment instead. He could not stop himself from crying as he watched the balloons soar skyward like souls ascending to heaven.

Facebook photos

In an effort to extend the reach of their search, Samantha's family created a Facebook page dedicated to finding her. As hoped, the "Please Help Find Samantha Koenig" site generated multitudes of leads, but it also spawned a slew of misinformation, including false rumors that Samantha's body had been found at numerous locations throughout the Anchorage area. The rumors and false reports only worked to hinder police investigative efforts as a time clock on the site continued to tick, keeping track of how long Samantha had been missing. As Detective Doll described it, the Facebook page turned up "thousands of leads," but most were dead ends or false information, which only ended up "wasting a lot of police resources."

As the days passed, although the Anchorage Police Department worked the case around the clock, James Koenig grew frustrated with their lack of progress and lack of communication. And much of the community shared Koenig's frustration.

APD spokesman Dave Parker continued trying to quell the growing unease among the public.

"Investigations take time," he said. "We're doing it in the most professional and expeditious manner possible."

On Valentine's Day, two weeks since the abduction, donations raised the reward for information leading to Samantha's return to $60,000. Yet, James Koenig felt in his heart that his daughter's abduction was not about money.

"The reward is really moot at this point," Koenig said, "because if it was about money, I'd have her back by now. I could offer a million dollars and I don't think that would change a thing."

The stress of trying to find his daughter and not even knowing whether she was alive had begun to take its toll on him.

"It's just been a roller coaster ride," Koenig said. "I feel like I'm going to find her, then I don't find her come midnight, and then 'crash.' The next day I'm just kind of in solitude and not real talkative."

Only his family and friends had kept him going, and kept him sane.

"They keep me out of that dark place I don't want to be in," he said solemnly.

(Tammie & Iz - December 7, 2000)

The man who placed the personal ad tells Tammie that his name is Israel or "Iz" for short. He is in the Army and stationed at Fort Lewis, a little less than ten miles away from her. He is 21-years old. He asks if she wants to talk over the phone, and she agrees, even though she knows that they are too different for anything serious to come of it.

To her surprise, when she calls him, the conversation comes easily. They talk for five hours, staying on the phone until nearly 4:00 in the morning. He tells her that his friends had put him up to placing the personal ad, and he asks if she would like to meet for drinks. She agrees to meet him a couple days later with the understanding that there will be no expectations. They will simply play it by ear.

They meet at noon on December 9 at Montezuma's, a Mexican restaurant in Tacoma. Tammie suggested meeting at the restaurant because she feels safe there, and it is only a mile or two from her house. She is intrigued about meeting Iz in person, but she is also guarded and she still does not think anything will come of it. When she sees him walk into the restaurant, his appearance reinforces her doubts. He is lanky and a bit awkward, plain-looking with a slender but athletic build. He comes across as "nerdy," an impression bolstered by his rectangular, wire-rimmed glasses, short, dark brown hair, and large, "somewhat protruding" nose. He wears black jeans, black boots, and – under a sheepskin Levi's jacket – a black t-shirt with the arms cut off.

Tammie is not attracted to him at first, but much to her surprise, when they start talking, the two of them hit it off quickly. There are none of the uncomfortable awkward silences that often occur when meeting someone for the first time. Something between them just seems to click. The drinks turn into a long lunch that stretches into a lengthy drive around the Tacoma area, followed by dinner at Applebee's and a movie.

Despite her initial reservations and doubts, Tammie finds herself attracted to Iz intellectually and physically. He is smart and engaging, and they have similar backgrounds. They both grew up poor as the older siblings in their families, and they had both turned their back on organized religion. They share similar interests in music and movies, heavy metal and zombie movies being favorites for both of them. Rage Against the Machine, Cold Chamber, and Slipknot are among their favorite bands, and they both enjoy Rob Zombie films such as The Devil's Rejects. They are also both fans of horror books, especially Dean R. Koontz novels.

The attraction increases after they kiss, and Tammie feels electricity in the air when they are together. At the end of the evening, Iz makes it clear that he wants to spend the night with her, but Tammie politely declines his suggestion. She assumes that he is just another solider wanting a one night stand.

When he calls her the next day, she is pleasantly surprised. She invites him to come over to her place, and he quickly shows up with a six-pack of beer. He stays the night and comes over nearly every day after that. Drinking is something else they both enjoy, and they jokingly refer to their relationship as a "two-month drinking one night stand." Jim Beam on the rocks is Iz's drink of choice.

With Iz, Tammie feels sexy and desirable. Iz is a passionate partner, the "best lover hands down" that Tammie has ever had, and sex becomes a central part of their relationship.

On January 28, 2001, Super Bowl Sunday, Tammie and Iz make a "sex slave" bet about the game. Iz teases her because she does not know much about football. While he studies the plays and knows all of the players, she picks who will win the game based on which team has better looking uniforms and players. She picks the Baltimore Ravens. He chooses the New York Giants.

When the Ravens win 34-7, Tammie claims her prize. She wants Iz to take a bubble bath with her and then give her a long massage, but they never make it to the massage part. It is the only time they have unprotected sex.

Iz is in the field with his Army unit when Tammie finds out that she *is pregnant. She calls him on his cell phone, and when he sees who is calling, he immediately knows why. He asks her to get an abortion, but she refuses. She tells him that he can forget about her and move on with his life, and that she will take care of the child herself. By the time the call ends, they have agreed to break up.*

Ten

On the morning of February 16, 2012, the man who murdered Samantha Koenig drove out of Dallas with the intention of robbing a small-town bank. After scouting an area in Aledo, Texas, and selecting a bank near the center of town, he decided to stage a diversion to draw the attention of local law enforcement. It would ensure that there would be less police around at the time of the actual robbery. He decided that a 3,500-square-foot home at 201 East Terrace Court in the Annetta South area of town would serve nicely for what he needed. The house and adjacent barn were about five miles from the bank, sufficiently far away for his purposes.

He had originally planned on abducting someone from an ATM, taking them to the house, and killing them, but he changed his mind and decided to burn the house down as a diversion instead. The large number of police that he had encountered during his time in Texas had impressed him enough to scrap thoughts of the abduction.

He pried open the back door of the house using a piece of steel he found in the garage, and then searched through the house for the next couple of hours looking for anything he might want to take. Before setting fire to the building, he opened all of the windows and made a trail of clothes and bedding leading into all of the rooms. Then he poured gas on the end of the clothes trail as he walked out the back door. He did the same thing to the adjacent barn to set it on fire.

As he drove away from the raging blaze, he stopped a neighbor and calmly asked for directions. The red-orange flames engulfing the house and barn were visible for miles, while the burning wood from the two structures popped, crackled, and hissed. Thick, black smoke poured from the flames, blanketing the air and blocking out the sky. While emergency vehicles responded to the scene, the arsonist stood by a church on a hill, watching through binoculars, pleased with a job well done.

The next day, the Parker County Fire Marshal's Office announced its findings about the cause of the fire.

"It's very unusual, very suspicious," Investigator Larry Padgett said. "There were two buildings separated by 40 yards, and both structures were involved when firefighters arrived, but there was no grass or vegetation burned between them. And it wasn't the result of radiant heat from one to the other."

He concluded that arson was to blame.

In Azle, another small Texas town, Samantha Koeing's killer parked his blue Kia Soul rental car a few blocks away from The National Bank of Texas, a bank he targeted due to its location. There were not many people around and there was easy access to major roads leading out of town. He put on a hardhat, glasses, and gloves, then placed an air respirator over his mouth to help conceal his face. The hardhat had human hair taped to the inside to further disguise his identity.

His preparations complete, he strode into the bank lobby brandishing the same .40 caliber handgun he had used for other bank robberies. After making his getaway, he stopped at a nearby gas station and filled his car's tank, watching with calm amusement as police vehicles sped by on their way to the bank.

On Sunday, February 18, the phantom fugitive returned his rental car to the Houston airport. He had put nearly 3,000 miles on it in six days. He arrived back in Anchorage in the early morning hours, having taken a red-eye flight from Texas. After arriving home, he checked on Samantha Koenig's body, which was still hidden in the shed. He had plans for the body, but he could not do anything else with it that weekend since his daughter was around.

On Monday the 19th, his daughter went to school, providing him the opportunity he needed to attend to the body, but since it had frozen solid, he had a hard time getting the body out of the garage cabinet. He had to remove the cabinet doors and dismantle the entire unit to free the body. A large amount of blood had leaked into the insulation of the cabinet floor from the stab wound on Samantha's back, so he had to tear up that area of flooring and dispose of it in the fireplace. The sleeping bag the body was wrapped in had become soaked with blood as well. He had to cut it up and throw the pieces into a jumbo garbage bag, along with Samantha's clothes and the tarp she had been wrapped in. Then it all went into the upstairs fireplace. As the last of the items disappeared in the flames, he returned to the shed and took everything out of it so that he could finish cleaning up. Using a bucket of hot water mixed with bleach, he mopped the shed's floor. Once it had dried, he put a 15 x 20 foot piece of plastic on the floor and then erected a table inside the shed.

After thawing out Samantha's body, he put it on the table, securing her arms up above her head by tying ropes to them and screwing the ropes to the wall of the shed. Then he had sex with Samantha's corpse. He was surprised to still feel warmth.

After he had finished, he returned to the house, leaving Samantha's body on the table. He knew that he had a lot to do since his girlfriend would be getting home the next day. He spent much of the rest of the day looking for a Polaroid camera, finally finding one at Target via an online search. He stopped by Target to purchase the camera after picking up his daughter from school, but the store did not carry any film for the camera. To get the film, he had to drive to a different Target in Wasilla that night after tucking his daughter into bed.

The next day, he picked up his girlfriend, Kimberly, at the airport, and for the next few days, he concentrated on various work tasks, but he also stopped by Walmart and purchased some women's make-up similar to the color and type that Samantha had in her purse. He picked up some fishing line and sewing needles at Walmart as well. Later, he found a stack of newspapers in a recycling dumpster behind Carr's grocery store. The papers were in chronological order from February 6 to February 20. He decided to use the February 13 edition for his ransom note.

He hoped that the women's cosmetics he bought at Wal-Mart would create the illusion that Samantha's lifeless body was actually alive. He spent three or four hours working on her make-up and posing her to make her the most life-like. The process was slow going because it took several layers of make-up to conceal the bruising and blood that had become visible under her skin. He had to use two or three tubes of foundation and then go over it with additional coloring. Even then, she looked like she had been painted, so he had to go back and add in some red color.

Her face presented a particular challenge. He taped it to provide some texture, but he had trouble getting rid of the expressionless features. He tried using Super Glue, but that did not work either. So he tried something else. Using the needles and fishing line that he had purchased, he sewed down between her eyebrows and up along the nose cartilage before coming out and going back up along the same path, pulling tight at the end to make it look like she was squeezing her eyes shut.

"She didn't look good," he later recalled. "I mean, her skin – you could start to see the blood under the skin and some bruising. She definitely didn't look alive. And so, yeah, it took me a long time."

Once he was satisfied with his handiwork, he used the Polaroid camera to take a test photo. After studying the photograph, he added more make up to Samantha's face and braided her hair to add to the illusion of life. Then he took another picture, and another, and another.

Although he needed to hold Samantha's head up, he did not want much of his arm showing in the photograph because he was afraid that law enforcement would notice a mole or other marking on his arm that could be used to identify him. By the fifth or sixth attempt, he achieved what he wanted.

Now that he had an adequate photograph, he needed a ransom note. Using a typewriter that he had purchased the day before at a local Salvation Army thrift shop, he typed up a draft. He wore latex gloves while typing to ensure that he would not leave any fingerprints. In the note, he mentioned how Samantha had tried to escape outside the coffee shop on Tudor and then – to throw investigators off the trail – he added that she had also nearly escaped "once in the desert."

He decided to ask for $30,000 as the ransom. He had been following the story of Samantha's abduction in news reports online and he was amazed to read about how much money had been donated to the reward fund. He directed that the ransom money be deposited into the bank account linked to the Credit Union 1 VISA debit card that he had taken from Samantha's truck. When he was satisfied with the ransom note, he sealed it in two Ziploc bags, one inside the other.

By February 21, the reward fund for Samantha's return had grown to over $65,000. Anchorage Police Department detectives continued to work nights and weekends interviewing hundreds of individuals and following up more than 350 leads. Yet, investigators remained in the dark about the identity of Samantha's abductor. Sergeant Slawomir Markiewicz emphasized that the APD's investigative efforts comprised a "continuous effort," but he could not point to a potential suspect in Samantha's disappearance.

"There may be theories that need to be talked about or examined," he said vaguely. "I don't want to say which one is the strongest, which one is the weakest."

Markiewicz downplayed the notion that the chances of finding Samantha alive continued to diminish with the passage of time.

"We haven't found any evidence that anything else happened to her. I think the main thing here is that there is no evidence to contradict that."

Meanwhile, James Koenig held tight to the belief that his only daughter might still be alive.

"I feel her in my heart," he said. "I know she's still alive. She's close. I just have to keep the hope and believe in what the police tell me, that they're doing everything they can."

Yet, he continued to grow frustrated with the apparent lack of progress in the case. Needing an outlet for his frustration, he took to social media and directed a plea and warning to his daughter's abductor, promising that he would hand over the reward money if Samantha was released unharmed, but also issuing a threat. He wrote on Facebook,

"I have resources, good and bad. I do not want to unleash the bad. I do not wish ill against you or yours, but if this does not end soon, you leave me no choice."

———————

(Tammie & Iz - 2001)

Tammie moves back to Neah Bay at the end of March to be closer to her family so that they can help her with the soon-to-be-coming baby. In early May, Iz calls. He tells her that he will be getting out of the Army in July and he wants to spend the weekend with her in Port Angeles.

During their weekend together, Iz opens up to her. He confesses that he has a 19-year-old fiancée in Colville whose father owns a cabinet-making business. He had planned on marrying her and taking over the business, but the news of Tammie's pregnancy has caused him to reconsider his future. He no longer wants to marry the girl in Colville. He wants to be with Tammie, and he promises her that he will do whatever it takes to make things up to her. The news sweeps over Tammie in a flood of emotions. She had missed Iz immensely since their break-up, and she finds herself agreeing to give their relationship another chance.

In July, Iz receives his honorable discharge from the Army. Tammie picks him up at the barracks and asks him to prove that he is serious about starting a new life with her. Iz does not hesitate. With Tammie watching, he calls his fiancée and tells her that he is not going to marry her. Then he calls his mother and gives her the same news. He says he realizes that he belongs with Tammie.

Iz is attracted to Tammie's independence and her carefree approach to life, and he never forgot how they had clicked right from the start. He also likes the fact that she does not care about his little white lies, such as saying that he had extra duty when he was really out drinking with friends.

Iz showers Tammie with attention and affection, doting on her, bringing her flowers and jewelry on a regular basis. As their relationship grows, observers often remark how much in love they look. Tammie falls in love with him and feels that they are "soulmates." He is friendly, intelligent, and funny, though he can be shy around people he does not know, and he has a social awkwardness at times. He seems uncomfortable when he is around too many people.

He is also prone to adopting a pompous, arrogant attitude, and he abhors materialistic people. He does not like Americans in general, or more specifically, the American way of life, which he views as promoting living on credit, joining the rat-race, and trying to keep up with the Joneses. His time serving overseas in the Army had profoundly influenced his world outlook and he had come to view Americans as spoiled and lazy.

Ironically, although he is a "control freak" who always thinks ahead and plans for the future, he also has an addictive personality, which is most evident in his tendency toward heavy drinking. A "highly functioning alcoholic," it is not uncommon for him to down a fifth of liquor, a bottle of wine, and a six-pack of beer in one evening. However, Tammie has her own addictions, so she never presumes to find fault with him for his.

One night while they are watching an episode of Dateline, a segment airs about Chevie and Cheyne Kehoe, white supremacist brothers who had been arrested in 1997 following a shoot-out with police after being pulled over for driving with an expired license plate. Chevie Kehoe was subsequently found guilty of three counts of murder for the 1995 killings of a gun dealer, his wife, and eight-year-old daughter in Arkansas.

As they watch the show, Iz casually mentions that he had grown up with the Kehoe brothers. After getting over her surprise, Tammie asks Iz what the Kehoes had been like when he knew them, but he does not want to talk about them and gives only vague comments in response. Sensing his reluctance to discuss his relationship with the Kehoes in any detail, Tammie does not press him about it further, but it remains something that always bothers her.

Eleven

On the morning of February 24, 2012, Samantha Koenig's killer woke up around 6:00 a.m., much earlier than normal, and drove his girlfriend's car to Connor's Bog Dog Park at the corner of Jewel Lake Road and International Airport Road. Guided by a dark sense of humor, he hid the ransom note and photograph under a missing dog flyer that was tacked to a pole near the park's entrance. The top of the flyer read, "Please Help Find Albert." After leaving the note, he returned to his house and spent the rest of the day with Kimberly. That night, he acted as the designated driver for Kimberly and some of her friends as they went bar hopping.

He had originally planned on waiting a few days before sending a text about the ransom note. He wanted to make sure that the tire tracks that he left in the snow were walked over or otherwise erased, but he convinced himself that the park had been busy enough for the tracks to have quickly been concealed. He was not worried about any shoe prints he might have left because he had already thrown away the shoes he wore. Concerned that the ransom note might fall out of its hiding place, he decided to go ahead and send the text.

After stopping at Carr's grocery store to pick up a case of beer for Kimberly and her friends, he pulled into the back corner of the parking lot, turned on Samantha's cell phone, and sent a text to her boyfriend's cell phone number: "Conner park sign under pic of albert aint she purty." He had planned on sending the text as a group message to all of the contacts on Samantha's phone, but there were too many people milling around the parking lot and he did not want to risk having someone notice him. After satisfying himself that the text went through, he removed the cell phone's battery and drove home.

Duane Tortolani was eating at Golden Corral with James Koenig when his cell phone chimed to announce that a new text had been received. It was the ransom text. After reading the message, he showed it to James, and the two hurried to Connor's Bog Park. James found the Ziploc bag under the lost dog flyer and immediately called the Anchorage Police Department, being careful not to touch the bag in case the kidnapper's fingerprints were on it.

A few hours after sending the text, the killer's curiosity about the ransom note got the best of him. He decided to go for a drive to see if it had been found. He headed down Wisconsin Street to the bohemian neighborhood of Spenard near the airport, and then drove by the entrance to the park. A crime scene van and several APD patrol cars were parked near the spot where he had hidden the note. He smiled in satisfaction of his own cleverness. To be as inconspicuous as possible, he kept driving past the park, careful not to call attention to himself by slowing down, before continuing on to Jewel Lake Road. When he reached Raspberry Road, he called Kimberly to check on her where-abouts, and then returned home.

Before long, he noticed that the body in the shed was beginning to smell. He would have to get rid of the evidence before the stench became noticeable to one of his neighbors. He thought about digging a hole in a snow bank in the backyard for temporary storage of the body, but decided against it. It would be better to find a permanent disposal site. He pulled the body off the table, took the table apart, cut up the plywood, and burned it.

Before beginning his grisly task, he placed visqueen polyethylene sheeting on the walls and floor of the shed. Using some wire as a tourniquet to keep the bleeding to a minimum, he did most of the cutting by hand using a yellow-handled DeWalt utility knife with a 25 millimeter disposable blade for the majority of the job. He needed a battery- powered Sawzall for a couple of the bigger cuts. He worked slowly, carefully to minimize the mess that would need to be cleaned up afterward. When the gory chore was done, he wiped everything down and removed the Sawzall blade so he could burn it later at the landfill. He put the body parts in a rolling tote bag before moving them into 55-gallon plastic garbage bags, triple bagging each load in two different bundles. Then he put the bags in the corner of the shed, where they would remain for several days until he was ready to take them to their final destination.

After analyzing the ransom note recovered from Connor Bog Park, Detective Doll called James Koenig into the police station to share it with him. The one-page ransom note included a photo of Samantha sprawled naked on a mattress with a copy of the February 13 edition of the *Anchorage Daily News* displayed beside her. The typed note demanded that $30,000 be deposited directly into Samantha's bank account, and stated that money would be withdrawn at regular intervals over the coming days in locations other than Alaska, advising: *I may not use the card much in ak due to small pop but as I will be leaving soon I will be using it all over.* The note also indicated that Samantha had been moved out of the state: *she did almost get away twice, once on tudor and once in the desert. Must be losing my touch.*

James noticed that Sam's hair appeared greasy or wet in the photograph and the tone of her skin color did not look right. Nevertheless, he was grateful to see that his missing daughter might still be alive.

The next day, members of the Anchorage community joined Samantha's family and friends at a benefit concert at the Time Out Lounge on Old Seward Highway. Seven bands were scheduled to perform. They named the event "Sam Stock," and the reward money for Samantha's safe return continued to grow. An earlier concert at the Top Hat Studio in east Anchorage had already boosted the reward fund to nearly $70,000.

———————

On February 27, he stopped by Walmart for some supplies. He purchased fishing line, hooks, lures, and other items that he needed for a trip which he would soon be taking, a trip on which fishing would be a secondary concern.

(Tammie & Iz - 2001-2002)

Tammie and Iz share a rental house on the Makah Indian Reservation across the street from her sister's home on Pine Street. The three-bedroom, one-bathroom house is in bad shape when they move in – practically "unlivable" at first – but Iz is good with tools and he fixes it up nicely.

Iz dotes on Tammie and Keaton, her 8-year-old son from a failed former marriage. Although Iz and Keaton are shy together at first, Keaton soon comes to regard him as the "best role model he had as a dad."

Iz often talks about growing up poor, including mentioning that he has disfigured toes due to having to wear shoes as a child that were too small for him. When Tammie tells him details about her own rough childhood, it brings them even closer.

From April 2001 to February 2002, Tammie's job requires her to travel at regular intervals, usually every three months, for up to five days at a time. During those trips, she keeps in touch with Iz, but gives no thought to keeping track of any travels he undertakes. She has no reason to keep tabs on him. After all, nothing about Iz suggests that he is anything more than he appears to be. On one occasion he remarks, "I'm a bad person," and another time he refers to himself as having a "black heart," but Tammie simply chalks such comments up to drinking too much.

There are some small changes about Iz that Tammie notices, though. He begins to grow out his hair and starts an online poker account using the name "Blackheart." He also starts listening exclusively to darker heavy metal music, such as Coal Chambers and Soil, whose lyrics deeply resonate with him. He even dedicates Soil's song, "Halo," to Tammie. When he brands an upside down cross on his chest and gets a pentagram tattooed on the back of his neck, Tammie figures that he is going through an angry or rebellious phase, the type many young men pass through on their way to their more mature personas.

Throughout their time together, Iz's attitude toward organized reli-

gion never wavers. He consistently dismisses and resents it. As his family's eldest son, Iz had taken the brunt of his parents' extreme religious views, especially those of his mother, Heidi. One day, Tammie stumbles across a journal that Iz had kept from his childhood. The journal contains pages and pages of scriptures copied in Iz's handwriting along with comments like "I had sinful thoughts today about my girlfriend."

Growing up, Iz had always been caught between a child's natural desire of pleasing his parents on the one hand, and finding his own path on the other. The imposing, almost abusive religious views of his parents inevitably took their toll on him. It seems to Tammie that he despised his parents, yet wanted their approval nonetheless. He comes to resent not just their religion, but any organized religion, and it spawns an unresolved anger that he carries inside of him.

Twelve

On February 29, five days after sending the ransom text, Samantha Koenig's murderer used her debit card to check whether the ransom money had been deposited into her bank account. Using Kimberly's SUV, he stopped at the Sea Galley restaurant parking lot across the street from the Alaska USA bank at 4000 Credit Union Drive. Wearing a black, hooded sweatshirt and black pants, he scurried across the street to the bank's ATM. He attempted to withdraw $600, but the transaction was denied because it exceeded the bank's daily $500 limit. What angered him more than the aborted withdrawal was the fact that ATM showed an account balance of only $5,000, not the $30,000 ransom he had demanded.

He considered sending a group text to all of Samantha's contacts stating that the ransom had gone up by $10,000 and that it would be the last message they would receive. He figured that would scare them into compliance, but he decided to wait until going out of state to send the text. It would be safer that way.

He returned to his car and drove away in search of another ATM. After spotting one at the Denali Alaskan Federal Credit Union on Minnesota Drive, he withdrew $500 from the account shortly before midnight, wearing gloves to avoid leaving fingerprints and donning glasses and a mask to conceal his face. Half an hour later, he withdrew another $500 from Samantha's account, this time using the Alaska USA bank at 7701 Debarr Road.

Over the days that followed, over 300 law enforcement officers worked the case while staking out all of the ATMs in the Anchorage area, some fifty locations in all. As investigators monitored his electronic path and stayed on his ATM trail, the unknown killer followed the Koenig case in the media, unable to resist posting in the online comments section of an *Anchorage Daily News* article about the case. In his comments, he pointed out that Crime Stoppers did not have any information about Samantha Koenig and that the FBI had not added her to the National Missing Persons database. On March 3 at 2:19 a.m., after several glasses of Jim Beam, he wrote: "Nothing surprises me anymore."

Elsewhere online, Chelsea Hoffman, a true crime blogger, posted a blog about psychic profiler Carla Baron's involvement in the Koenig case. Baron had asserted her belief that Samantha was still alive.

I see Samantha Koenig alive, Hoffman quoted Baron as saying. *She is cooperating with her captor for self-preservation, and I told her father James this morning how very smart she is to do just that.*

On March 6, Hoffman posted another blog entitled, "Samantha Koenig Shocking Exclusive: Sex, Drugs and Theft Before Woman Went Missing." In her new posting, Hoffman recounted a conversation she had with Tammie Counts, mother of Christopher Bird. According to Counts, Chris and Samantha had known each other for about six months prior to her abduction, during which time Samantha frequently came over to Counts's house and talked with her, often staying for dinner. On several occasions, Samantha confided to her about having problems with her boyfriend and father and disclosed that she had used heroin with her mother for a period of time but had been able to kick the habit before becoming addicted. Counts also claimed that Chris and Samantha had engaged in consensual sexual intercourse one night at her house, and she continued to insist that her son had nothing to do with Samantha's disappearance. She pointed out that, at the time of her disappearance, Chris was home enjoying a meal of fried chicken, mashed potatoes, and green beans with his family, a fact corroborated by several witnesses.

"If my son had anything to do with this," Counts asserted, "he'd be sitting in jail right now. We told the police that we'll give lie detector tests, DNA, whatever you want."

Michael Pederson, Samantha's step-brother, supported Counts's account, writing on Facebook that Samantha had told him that she made up the story about being raped by Christopher Bird because she did not want her boyfriend to know that she had cheated on him.

On the same day that Hoffman posted her latest blog, the man who murdered Samantha Koenig caught a flight from Anchorage to Las Vegas, where he rented a white Ford Focus from Avis Rent A Car and drove to Dallas, Texas. On March 7, he drove north into Arizona. Just before 10:00 p.m., in the small town of Willcox in southern Arizona, he parked by an ATM at the Western Bank on West Rex Allen Drive near Interstate 10. Wearing several layers of clothing to make himself look heavier, as well as gloves and a Halloween mask resembling the killer from the *Scream* movies, he inserted Samantha Koenig's debit card into the machine, typed in the code scratched on the card, and withdrew $400. Ninety minutes later, he tried withdrawing another $400 from the account at an ATM at the Western Bank on Main Street in Lordsburg, New Mexico. After the transaction was declined because it would exceed the daily withdrawal limit, he withdrew $80 and drove away, disappearing like a ghost in the desert night.

Although the FBI received remote electronic notification of the debit card being used, the man was long gone by the time agents arrived at the locations minutes later. However, the initial disappointment of having missed him again soon gave way to renewed hope. Video footage from one of the bank's wide angle surveillance cameras had captured the blurry image of a white sedan driving away and heading back towards I-10. Investigators now had video of the man's rental car, and some quick work by FBI analysts culminated in an identification of the car as a white 2012 Ford Focus.

Emboldened by a psychologically constructed cocoon of invincibility, Samantha Koenig's killer had underestimated or misjudged the range of the bank's exterior security camera. Or perhaps he had simply reached the point of no longer caring whether he was caught. Whatever the reason, this would prove to be a critical lapse of judgment, one that could provide the key to solving not only the Samantha Koenig case, but another baffling disappearance over 3,000 miles away.

"We chased lead after lead after lead," Lt. Dave Parker of the APD would later say. "Every lead led us nowhere. It was tough, really tough."

APD officer Jeff Bell echoed Parker's appraisal.

"We had no idea who he was," Bell said.

"There is no clue until he started using that debit card," Parker pointedly admitted.

On March 8, Sergeant Slawomir Markiewicz, the head of the Anchorage Police Department's Homicide Unit, lifted the spirits of Samantha's family and friends by announcing that the police had reason to believe that Samantha was still alive.

"I'm privy to the details of the investigation," Markiewicz said, "and I believe that she's alive."

Markiewicz's public revelation rekindled James Koenig's simmering hopes.

"I believe that's the mind set we all have to keep," he said anxiously. "I mean, there's nothing that says she isn't alive."

On March 9, around 11:20 p.m., Samantha's killer withdrew $480 from an ATM at the Houston Community Bank in Humble City, Texas, just across from the airport. While in town, he stopped at the local Avis car rental office and requested a new vehicle. With a different car, he would have blended back into anonymity and disappeared, and law enforcement's only solid lead would have turned into a wild goose chase.

But Fate, or the hand of God, intervened and handed investigators an incredible break. The man who had stayed a step ahead of the police received another car, but due to limited inventory on hand, the Avis agent gave him the same make and model vehicle that he had before. Not only that, it was the same color too. When he pulled out of the rental car parking lot with a new vehicle, he was still driving a white Ford Focus.

Meanwhile, the FBI issued an alert to Texas law enforcement, advising them to be on the lookout for a white 2012 Ford Focus. After reviewing the alert, Texas Ranger Steve Rayburn passed it along to his fellow Rangers.

Two days later, Samantha's killer headed toward Grand Prairie, Texas, to attend his sister's wedding. Just before 11:30 p.m. on March 11, he made another $480 withdrawal, this time from the People's State Bank on Highway 59 in Shepherd, Texas, about half-way between Houston and Lufkin. Then he drove for another hour or so before checking into a Quality Inn & Suites at 4306 South First Street in the town of Lufkin, about 120 miles northeast of Houston.

The following day, in Nacogdoches, northeast of Wells, he attended his sister's wedding ceremony along with approximately 75 other guests. While visiting with family members, he was confronted about his disbelief in the teachings of the Church of Wells. One of them asked a pointed question.

"When did you first decide that you were going to hate God?"

"I don't believe in God," he responded coldly, before stepping out onto the porch to smoke a cigarette. His sister-in-law followed him outside.

"You know," she said, touching him gently on the shoulders, "God will forgive you for however you have sinned."

His face had settled into a momentary expression of sadness, but the sensation of her hand on his shoulder startled him, and abruptly he pulled away. The moment of vulnerability had been destroyed by a simple touch.

"You don't know what I've been through," he proclaimed with a tone of accusation. "I have to drink every day to forget what I've done."

His eyes slowly narrowed and a shadow seemed to fall across his face.

"You don't know the depths of darkness that I've been to," he said sadly. "You don't know what I've done."

Jacob Gardner, the charismatic leader of the Church of Wells, presented the sermon during the wedding ceremony. As Gardner delved deeper into his sermon, it shifted to an attack on Samantha's killer's atheism. The man glared at Gardner and stood up as a wave of anger swept over him.

"Your gospel has no grounding in truth," he bellowed indignantly.

Silence enveloped the gathering as he stepped toward Gardner, fixing him with an ominous stare while his mouth broke into an icy smile.

"Not everyone shares your beliefs," he muttered bitterly, as Gardner nervously backed away.

The man's resentment of his sister's church was merely the latest manifestation of his rejection of the Christian beliefs of his parents, a spiritual and psychological struggle he was determined to end according to his own terms.

(Tammie & Iz - 2002)

Tammie and Iz enjoy watching TV together, listening to music, and playing trivia games. On weekends, they regularly have friends over.

Whenever Tammie asks Iz about his relationship with his mother, he usually avoids talking about it. He always seems to crave his mother's approval, but it remains a sore spot throughout their relationship. The few times that Tammie speaks with Iz's mother, Heidi, on the telephone, she finds her to be very judgmental. Heidi uses religion as a weapon, quoting passages from the Bible as support for judging other people. Tammie eventually concludes that although he has many anti-government beliefs, Iz had signed up for a stint in the military as an act of rebellion against his parents.

As her pregnancy progresses into its late term, Tammie finds herself working more and more. The demands of her job as the Early Childhood Development Manager for the reservation require her to work a lot of overtime, and that's where she is when she goes into labor.

Iz is "a mess" when he hears that her water broke. Despite his boasting about having "birthed a lot of lamb" with his family when he was growing up, Iz "fell apart" when the time came for the birth of his own child. He rushes Tammie to the hospital in Port Angeles, and at 4:30 a.m. on Halloween 2002, Sarah Keyes is born. Despite his nervousness, Iz stays in the delivery room the entire time.

Named after her mother's and grandmother's middle name, Sarah has a profound effect on Iz.

"I saw his life change when she was born," Tammie later recalls.

Thirteen

On March 13, 2012, at approximately 3:30 a.m., the man who had raped and murdered Samantha Koenig stepped out onto the balcony of room 215 of the Lufkin Quality Inn to smoke a cigarette. He spied a Lufkin Police Department patrol car moving slowly through the motel's parking lot and watched warily as the police car idled near his rental car. Just as he started getting concerned, the cruiser resumed its journey through the parking lot and drove away.

A few hours later, at 7:30 a.m., Texas Highway Patrol Corporal Bryan Henry approached the Quality Inn on his usual route through Lufkin. A long-time member of the patrol with over two decades of law enforcement experience, Henry had received the BOLO from Ranger Rayburn regarding a white Ford Focus, and he had been actively searching for the vehicle ever since. He slowed down and spotted a car matching the vehicle's description as he pulled into the hotel parking lot. After running the plate and pulling the car's registration, Henry called Rayburn to brief him about what he had found.

After instructing Henry to keep his distance until they could better assess the situation, Rayburn sped to the Quality Inn accompanied by FBI agent Deb Gannoway. Upon their arrival at the motel, Gannoway walked over to the car and noticed a bar-code sticker on the back passenger window identifying it as a rental vehicle. A database search of the license plate confirmed the vehicle's status as a rental, and an inquiry with the front desk manager revealed that Room 215 had been rented by "Elijah Keyes" for the time period of March 9 through March 13. Rayburn and the others hastily took up surveillance positions around the parking lot.

Around 11:30 a.m., they watched as the occupant of Room 215 walked to the parking lot, placed some items in the trunk of his car, and drove away. Corporal Henry trailed at an inconspicuous distance behind him. As the man drove down Highway 59, Henry noticed that he was going three miles over the speed limit. That was all Henry needed. He activated his cruiser's emergency lights and followed the rental car as it pulled into the parking lot of the Cotton Patch Café near the Davy Crockett National Forest.

At 11:45 a.m., diners at the Cotton Patch were enjoying its specialty of chicken-fried steak as a white Ford Focus turned into the parking lot trailed by a Lufkin police cruiser. Customers sitting outside of the restaurant watched as Corporal Henry walked cautiously toward the Ford's driver's side window.

As he stepped up to the window, Henry saw that the driver was wearing a sleeveless tank top and blue jeans. Sunglasses concealed his eyes.

"Good morning, sir," Henry said, "could I see your license and registration, please?"

"Good morning, officer," the man replied. "Here you go," he said, handing over his license. "Was I speeding?"

The question hung in the air unanswered as Henry examined the driver's license. The license had been issued in Alaska and the photograph on the license matched the face of the man behind the wheel. The man's name was Israel Keyes.

After seeing that the license had been issued in Alaska, Henry knew that he should radio Ranger Rayburn for backup.

"Sit tight a second, Mr. Keyes," Henry said before walking back to his patrol car.

After returning to the rental car, Henry asked Keyes a series of questions focusing on why he was in the area. Though at first pleasant and cooperative, as Henry continued to question him, Keyes became increasingly agitated and refused to allow Henry to inspect his wallet or the vehicle. Henry also noticed that, despite the cool weather, Keyes had begun to sweat profusely.

Satisfied that Keyes's appearance matched that of the individual caught on ATM video using Samantha Koenig's debit card, and that the Ford Focus matched the vehicle seen on bank video footage, Henry handcuffed Keyes and placed him under arrest. During a subsequent search of Keyes's vehicle, officers found a gun, a dye-stained roll of bills from a bank robbery, the mask Keyes wore while withdrawing cash from ATMs, and most crucially of all, Samantha Koenig's debit card and cellphone.

The clever killer who idolized Ted Bundy and thought that he was too smart to get caught, had made a careless mistake, just as his hero had done two decades before.

| Israel Keyes

Ranger Rayburn deemed the arrest of Israel Keyes the result of "divine intervention," while Sgt. Markiewicz of the APD attributed it to "methodical, meticulous police work."

"This wasn't the result of luck," Markiewicz boasted.

But he back-tracked on the prior comments he had made about believing Samantha to still be alive.

"We investigated as if she's alive. We haven't found her. We don't know what happened with her. We're concerned. We don't know if she's alive."

Jeff Bell, a 17-year veteran and member of the APD's SWAT team, expressed the general reaction of his fellow officers to Keyes's arrest.

"Elation," Bell explained. "We had no idea who he was until that moment."

Lt. Dave Parker agreed.

"It was a huge, huge relief to have our arms around this and know this was the guy," Parker said. "We had been barking up every wrong tree in our community, and suddenly we had the guy."

Just before news of the arrest was announced to the public, Detective Doll called Samantha's father to let him know that a suspect had been taken into custody. An exhausted, but elated James Koenig prayed that the arrest would mean a happy ending to what had been a living nightmare.

"I hope it is the guy," he said. "I hope my daughter can come home now."

He felt conflicting emotions after learning more about the arrest.

"I feel several emotions," he said, "I don't know how to explain them. I'm happy they got the guy. But I'm worried that if he was working by himself, where's my daughter?"

Others shared the concern about a lack of resolution.

"It's still not the ending," said Melanie Ornelas, a Common Grounds employee. "She's still missing. It doesn't really bring closure."

And Peggy Giles, a friend of the Koenig family, stressed the disturbing nature of Keyes's arrest.

"It was just shocking," she explained. "The reason this crime was more shocking than most was the randomness of the way he picked his victim."

Meanwhile, an APD SWAT team wearing body armor and brandishing shotguns executed a search warrant of Keyes's home on Spurr Lane. Among the items they seized was the trailer he used for his carpentry business, a photograph of Bill and Lorraine Currier, and a Burlington newspaper article about the Curriers' disappearance that was saved on Keyes's computer.

Doll and Bell were quickly dispatched to Texas, catching the soonest red-eye flight. After landing, they drove directly to the courthouse where Keyes awaited arraignment, and hurried to an interview room where he sat handcuffed at a table. They both felt something ominous, but difficult to describe, when they walked into the room.

"He definitely gave you a chilling feeling, Bell recalled. "Detective Doll and I both had that sense. The hair on the back of your neck stands up. We knew Samantha likely did not have a good outcome."

Doll showed Keyes the evidence that Anchorage investigators had amassed since his arrest, evidence which clearly connected him to Samantha Koenig's abduction. Then she brought out the ransom note and placed it on the table in front of him.

"The first few times I read this, I thought that whoever wrote it must be a monster," Doll told him. "But the more I read it, the more I understood that monsters aren't born. They're made. And that people who start off on one path can end up on a radically different path because of things that people do to them. And I knew that whoever wrote this had a story to tell."

She paused and looked him in the eye.

"So what's your story?" she asked.

Keyes smiled politely.

"I can't help you," he replied.

She pressed him for information about Samantha's location, trying to appeal to him as the father of a little girl, evoking James Koenig's anguish in not knowing whether his daughter was dead or alive. Keyes seemed briefly affected by Doll's plea, but the moment quickly passed, and he stared back at her with cold, lifeless eyes.

"There's nothing I can do to help you," he told her matter-of-factly.

Back in Alaska, the news of Keyes's arrest universally stunned his neighbors.

"They're very quiet people, very friendly," said next- door neighbor Lorina Warren. "He works a lot," she added.

Russell Gunderson had never actually met Keyes, but had frequently seen him in the neighborhood, and never noticed anything odd or unusual about him.

"Nothing suspicious at all," Gunderson said, "except for that he worked hard. You know, he was always on the go."

Neighbor Tom McMillian similarly described Keyes as quiet and polite, and recalled how Keyes had been making improvements to the Spurr Lane house since moving in several years earlier. Keyes had sometimes used electric saws and other equipment in his yard, occasionally at night, and threw a few small parties each year, but McMillian remembered nothing else remarkable about him.

"I would be pretty surprised if he's involved with it," McMillian concluded.

An employee at nearby Spenard Builders Supply recalled Keyes as always being pleasant and cheerful, and Paul Adelman, an Anchorage attorney who had hired Keyes to help construct an apartment off the DeSarah Park Strip, described him as, "reliable, unfailingly polite, and responsive. I never got any bad, weird, scary, odd vibe from him in any way, shape, or form," Adelman said.

In fact, Adelman had been so impressed by Keyes's work that he recommended him to friends.

"He was absolutely honest and reliable and a person who was, in my opinion, utterly trustworthy, Adelman declared. "As far as I'm concerned, Israel is as honest as the day is long."

Even former friends and colleagues in Neah Bay remembered him as being very normal.

"He would tell me about his days in the armed services and the parties they had," said Jim Thompson. "He would lovingly talk about his daughter, or tell me when he'd been up late because she was sick."

David Kanters, a friend and coworker of Kimberly Anderson, was shocked to learn about the accusations against Keyes.

"He seemed totally normal," Kanters said. "He was quiet; he was more reserved, I guess, but you never would have picked him out for doing something like this. In no sense of the word was he in any way weird. He had everyone fooled. *That* is the scary part. He came across as a nice, normal guy."

Perhaps no one was as shocked at the news of Keyes's arrest as Heather Andrews. She and her husband had friends who knew Keyes's girlfriend, and through those shared friends, the Andrews hired Keyes in 2011 and again in 2012 to do some remodeling work and construct additions to their house. Keyes had done similar work for a handful of doctors in the area, and ended up spending several months at the Andrews' house doing the work, including a large part of the summer of 2011.

The man who introduced himself as "Izzy" seemed to have a warm and friendly personality, and he brought his daughter with him every day during the summer. Heather Andrews spent time teaching her how to sew and make bread while Keyes worked on the house. Andrews had heard Keyes's girlfriend did not help him much with parenting since she did not want kids, and she was struck by what a "devoted" father he appeared to be. She could tell that he had a genuine love for his daughter. Andrews thought Keyes was absolutely "adorable" with his daughter, and he told her that he had "saved" his daughter from her mother, who was a chronic drug abuser.

An industrious worker, Keyes had always been on time. If he said that he would be there at 9:00 a.m. on Tuesday, he would show up at

8:55 a.m. ready to work. He had always been "true to his word" in dealing with Andrews, and she could not help befriending him.

"He was very likeable," she said.

She remembered that he had talked about growing up in a "religious commune," and yet said that he was not very religious.

"Religion poisons people," Keyes had told her.

Andrews was struck by how strong he was considering his thin build.

"He was as strong as a bull," she recalled. "He could carry a beam over his shoulder without apparent effort. He had strength that had elegance. It seemed superhuman."

Andrews had observed, however, that Keyes seemed to change between 2011 when he first worked for her, and the second time in 2012 about a week before Samantha Koenig's abduction. He had grown noticeably moody, irritable, and quiet, and he often seemed grumpy or depressed. He even looked different, showing up disheveled and messy during the 2012 project. Their previously amicable discussions turned into very short conversations, and he would rarely make eye contact. One of the sole exceptions occurred when she was watching him through the kitchen window while he carried something across the yard. As she watched him walk, he suddenly looked over and fixed her with a strange stare. It gave her a creepy feeling, like he was looking into her very soul.

Keyes's peculiar changes had led Andrews believe that he was drinking too much. She grew so concerned about him that when he failed to show up one day – something highly out of character – she went to his house to check on him. She knocked on his door, but no one answered, so she knocked again, much louder. After a lengthy delay, Keyes appeared at the door, reeking of alcohol.

"Izzy, what's going on with you?" Andrews asked worriedly. "Are you okay? Whatever it is, we can get you some help if you need it."

"No, I'm fine," he replied, his voice monotone and distant. "I'm okay, I just get depressed in winter," he said with a sigh. "The winters are so long here."

She reached out and gave him a motherly hug, but he just stood there, his arms hanging rigidly at his sides. At that moment, she realized that he was emotionally empty.

"It felt like there was nobody there," she explained.

He eventually put his arms around her, but only after a long, awkward pause, as if it had finally dawned on him that reciprocating the embrace was what he was supposed to do.

Before she left, he mentioned that he was planning on moving away from Alaska and going back down to the Lower 48. About a week later, he came back to her house and finished his work.

Andrews shivered as she recalled standing with Keyes, hugging him, no more than twenty feet from the shed where, just a few days later, he would rape Samantha Koenig and strangle her to death.

Still, Andrews had a hard time reconciling the hard-working, devoted father she had known with the cold-blooded killer authorities alleged him to be.

"I didn't believe he killed her for the first month after it was announced," she said later. She felt like her trust had been betrayed, and the revelation that someone she had grown so fond of had so skillfully hidden such an evil side of his personality turned her world upside down. She no longer felt safe, and she suffered nightmares for months. Her experience with Keyes even caused her to question her own instincts.

"I was a nurse for 25 years," she explained, almost apologetically. "I always had a really good sense about people, but I never had any idea about him."

PART II: Dealing With The Devil

"I have sworn thee fair, and thought thee bright, Who art as black as hell, as dark as night"

Shakespeare -- Sonnet CXLVII

Fourteen

Tammie Hawkins was already in a low place when she learned of Keyes's arrest. She was depressed, nearly suicidal in a Port Angeles hotel room, when her sister called to tell her that she had seen a story on television about the arrest. The news shook Tammie to her core, but ironically also brought her back into a better frame of mind.

"It probably saved my life," she later reflected. "It woke me up – I had given up on life."

Tammie quickly made arrangements to fly to Texas to get Sarah, who had been with Iz for his sister's wedding. Tammie traveled to Dallas with Iz's sister, Charity, and met up with his mother, Heidi, who had temporary supervision of Sarah. It was the first time that Tammie met Heidi in person, and she equated it to stepping back in time to an old Quaker home. Heidi's deeply religious worldview was impossible to miss. She even tried to talk Tammie into letting Sarah stay with her in Texas so she could become a part of The Church of Wells. But Tammie was not about to let Sarah be brainwashed. She politely declined Heidi's suggestion.

Within a week of Iz's arrest, Tammie received a visit from two FBI agents who appeared at her house unannounced. They asked a lot of general questions about Iz, such as whether she knew anything quirky about him from his past, but they also had more specific, seemingly arcane ones, such as whether Iz knew how to French braid hair. In all, Tammie spent hours being interviewed by the FBI and, later, Iz's defense attorneys. The defense attorneys warned her not to talk to the FBI, while the FBI agents assured her that they were only trying to help her. The whole thing made her head spin. She wanted to be helpful, but came away utterly confused as to "who the bad guys were."

She recalled one recent event which had not seemed significant at the time, but that now stood out as indicative of Iz's psychological state and frame of mind during the weeks leading up to his arrest. Shortly before noon on February 20, she had received a text message from her frightened daughter. Sarah had found Iz passed out in the living room with a knife stuck in the coffee table, and she could not get him to wake up. The living room couch and curtains were cut up as well, apparently through the use of the knife. Tammie did her best to calm Sarah down and hoped that Iz was simply sleeping off another drinking bout. She left him a message to call her when he sobered up.

She had not heard from him until that evening. When he finally called, he had said that Sarah was simply overreacting, and he assured her that everything was fine. Tammie did not believe him since he had recently told her that he was depressed and that Sarah was the only reason he got out of bed most mornings. He had also confided that he and Kimberly had been having relationship problems for nearly a year. They were no longer having sex and Kim would sometimes sleep at a friend's house after they had a fight. Iz had hoped that things would get better when Sarah came to live with them, but nothing improved. If anything, Sarah's arrival had adversely affected the relationship because Kim seemed to resent the time he spent with Sarah. Kim had never wanted to have children because she enjoyed traveling, and her job as a medical provider for remote oil production facilities regularly kept her on the road.

On Wednesday, March 14, FBI Special Agent Steve Payne directed the filing of a Criminal Complaint in the United States District Court for the District of Alaska, alleging the federal crime of Access Device Fraud against Keyes.

The next day, Keyes appeared in federal district court for the Eastern District of Texas in Beaumont, Texas, for a Rule 5 hearing to address the removal of his case from Texas to Alaska. He had the legal right to have a preliminary hearing within fourteen days of his first court appearance to determine whether probable cause existed to warrant pursuing criminal proceedings, but after seeing the evidence that investigators had gathered against him, Keyes agreed to waive his rights and have his case transferred to the Federal District of Alaska for trial. After receiving the waiver, United States Magistrate Judge Zack Hawthorn remanded Keyes to the custody of the U.S. Marshal for his return to Alaska.

Even as Keyes waived his right to a preliminary hearing, detectives from the Anchorage Police Department were conducting searches and serving warrants in Texas as part of an "unprecedented number of detectives" working on the Samantha Koenig case. Meanwhile in Anchorage, James Koenig made it clear that his daughter had no prior connection to Keyes.

"This was, in my eyes, a random abduction. This was nothing to do with me, her, anyone in my family, no one's background, none of that. This guy went and stole a kid out of a coffee shop."

On March 22, based on Keyes's use of the debit card stolen from Samantha, a federal grand jury in the United States District Court for the District of Alaska returned an indictment against him for one count of Access Device Fraud.

On March 26, U.S. Marshals arrived in Anchorage with their cargo from the federal facility in Beaumont, Texas, and they delivered Keyes without incident to his new residence in an Anchorage jail. The next day, Keyes made his initial appearance in Alaska federal court before Judge John Roberts on the charge of access device fraud, pleading not guilty to pilfering a bank account with a stolen debit card. Showing no emotion, Keyes glanced around at the full gallery of twenty onlookers as he entered the courtroom. Clean-cut with his hair combed back, Keyes told Judge Roberts that he did not have the financial ability to afford his own attorney. In response, the judge appointed a public defender to represent him.

The next day, James Koenig posted a message to the community on the "Please Help Find Samantha Koenig" Facebook page, thanking everyone for their support, but imploring them to "please be patient, let the FBI, police, and U.S. Attorneys do their jobs, and hopefully get this guy talking."

Indeed, getting Keyes to talk would be the only hope for finding Samantha Koenig.

On March 31, 2012, investigators finally learned the heart-rending fate of Samantha Koenig. With his court-appointed attorney present, Keyes met with Kevin Feldis and Frank Russo of the United States Attorney's Office, as well as Jeff Bell and FBI Special Agent Steve Payne. Keyes told the team of investigators that he would give them some information about what happened to Samantha but would not "go into the whole story, blow for blow." He freely described how he had abducted her from the Common Grounds coffee stand, taken her to his shed, and obtained her debit card. But when they asked him whether she was alive at the time he left Alaska, he became coy, hinting that while he would be open to sharing more specifics eventually, he would not "tell the whole story today." Keyes insisted that he would divulge all of the details of what he had done to Samantha only if Detective Doll was there to hear them.

Bell asked Keyes why he specifically wanted to tell his story to Detective Doll.

"Because that's the way I am," he answered smugly.

Feldis, the lead federal prosecutor, wanted more.

"That's fine, we understand you're not going to tell us everything," Feldis explained, "but the one thing I do need to know before I leave here today is *how* you killed her."

"Why?" Keyes responded coolly. "It doesn't really matter how it happened. I'm saying that, 'yes,' I was responsible."

"Okay, so you are responsible for what?" Feldis continued. "I need you to tell me."

"For her being deceased," Keyes replied.

"So, you killed her?"

"Yes," Keyes acknowledged with a slight tone of annoyance, but then added, "I'll tell you everything you want to know. I'll give it blow by blow if you want. I have lots more stories to tell."

Silence filled the room as the meaning of the cryptic words "lots more stories" dawned on the representatives of the three law enforcement agencies. Keyes paused a moment to read their faces. Though pleased with their startled reaction, he warned the investigators that he would only tell those stories in bits and pieces. He wanted to make sure that they would handle the information discreetly and not drag his name through the mud in the media.

"My concern right now is that I want to see what happens. I'd rather not see my name attached to it. No *'Dismembered body found in the lake. Israel Keyes believed to be responsible.'* I don't want to see that yet."

Aside from not wanting his name publicly linked to any murder, he also needed time to get used to the fact that he was actually talking to someone about the things he had done. More importantly, he still had to come to terms with the fact that all of the people who he had fooled over the years would now know the truth about him. His false identity, meticulously crafted and maintained for so many years, would now disappear, and his true nature, so carefully kept hidden, would be unveiled for all to see.

"Call me crazy," Keyes continued, "but I've got to get used to the idea that everybody's going to know that I'm not who they thought I was. I've got to get used to that. It feels weird to talk about it. I've never talked about any of this stuff before."

He elaborated on the precondition to his cooperation: any information he provided had to be tightly controlled and limited in the extent of its release.

"There are ways you can let the media know what's going on without saying I'm the one who's responsible. I mean, eventually, everyone's going to know. But if I feel like you're doing the best you can to keep this – the impact on people I know and my family – to a minimum then, like I say, I've got other stories."

Feldis tried fishing for information about the "other stories" one last time.

"Are there any other people that you're responsible for the death of?" he prodded.

Keyes gave him a long, chilling look.

"I can't answer that," he finally replied. "I mean, like I say, we need to tackle one thing at a time."

He toyed with his interrogators by alluding to other murders.

"There is more to that story, there's a *lot* more to that story," he teased. "Like, why I did things the way I did them and the timeline. Because as you know, it's been going on for a while."

Before ending the interview, Keyes stressed that if they needed anything else from his house or shed, they should get it discreetly so as not to harass or inconvenience his girlfriend. The door having been opened, Feldis seized the opportunity to step through it.

"Do we have your consent to that house, to that trailer, to take any items that we – that law enforcement – want?" he asked.

"Yeah, take the whole shed," Keyes answered without hesitation. "Go for it. I just don't want to hear about you questioning her again."

Then he said something that would intrigue the investigators ever afterward.

"I can tell you right now there is no one who knows me – or who has ever known me – who knows anything about me, really. They're going tell you something that does not line up with anything I tell you because I'm two different people, basically. And the only person who knows about what I'm telling you – the kinds of things I'm telling you – is me."

The group of interviewers exchanged inquisitive glances, and then Russo spoke up.

"How long have you been two different people?" he asked incredulously.

Keyes gave a slight giggle before responding.

"A long time," he said proudly. "Fourteen years."

On the evening of March 31, FBI agents executed a second search warrant at the home Keyes shared with Kimberly Anderson. Around 10:00 p.m., approximately one dozen plain-clothed FBI agents arrived outside the blue single-family residence on Spurr Lane. A flat-bed truck pulled up near the driveway and unloaded a forklift. After shoveling snow from the roof of the 6-foot by 8-foot metal storage shed at the front of the driveway, a forklift operator picked up the green trimmed shed and backed slowly down the driveway before depositing the shed onto the back of the flatbed truck. The shed in which Keyes had murdered Samantha Koenig was soon on its way to the FBI's Anchorage office.

FBI spokesperson Eric Gonzalez declined to tell reporters why the shed was being taken, saying only that the seizure related to the Koenig case and that the FBI and Anchorage Police Department were working together on the case.

The next day, April 1, Keyes met again with many of the same investigative personnel – Feldis, Payne, Russo, and Bell – but this time APD Detective Monique Doll joined the group, as Keyes had requested.

After the preliminary greetings and re-advisement of his rights,

Keyes reiterated his condition that the specific details he would be sharing about Samantha Koenig's murder not be shared with the media or otherwise made available to the public.

"Before I go into anything, one thing I'm concerned about is that some of the details I tell you are going to be very graphic, and I don't want to hear about them being in the media," he said, before elaborating on the reason for his concerns.

"I'm trying to spare my family and people who know me the depth of, I guess you could say, the double life I have."

"Understood," Feldis assured him.

Keyes continued.

"If you expect me to say anything at any point in the future about anything else, whether it's this or anything, then that's going to hinge directly on what I perceive that you're portraying to the media."

Feldis attempted to assuage Keyes's concerns.

"Look, we're not out here to horrify anybody. We have respect for the public. I think that's what you're saying, right? You know, they don't need to hear all the details."

"That's my concern," Keyes replied, "that the media actually likes that stuff and the public does, too, whether you want to believe it or not. There's a lot of people who will want to hear all that."

Now Detective Doll addressed the issue as well:

I get what you're saying – people are voyeurs. People want to know the dirty little details, and this has been one of the most controlled releases of information – this case more so than any other case that's ever been worked by the Anchorage Police Department, we've done a better job at controlling outflow of information and we will continue to do so.

There's no reason for us to put the dirty little details about Samantha's death in the newspaper. There is also no reason for us to tell her father or anybody else the dirty little details – nothing that can get back to your family. The only people that need to know it are the investigators, you already know it, the attorneys, and eventually the judge. So I have no intention of releasing any details because it is only going to harm people, it's not going to help anybody. It's going to satisfy a sick curiosity and I'm not interested in that.

Keyes considered Doll's statement for a few moments. Apparently satisfied by her explanation, Keyes told the investigators that he would give them the location of Samantha's body because he believed that the FBI would figure it out anyway by analyzing his home computer. After all, he had only downloaded and printed information about one lake.

(Tammie & Iz - 2002)

Tammie and Iz are both excited beyond expression about the birth of their daughter. Tammie has always wanted a little girl and Iz has embraced the notion of becoming a parent. But as much joy as baby Sarah's arrival brings them, it also creates a lot of stress in their marriage. Sarah develops asthma and contracts RSV, a potentially dangerous viral respiratory infection, when she is just eight months old. Tammie and Iz sometimes fight over how best to handle Sarah's medical issues. Iz is anti-doctor and anti-immunization, while Tammie feels that they should get Sarah the best medical attention possible.

Despite their disagreements about Sarah's medical care, Tammie appreciates that Iz is such an attentive father. He is always willing to help out with feeding or changing her, and often takes the lead in doing so. He is, Tammie noticed, "definitely family oriented." He is a "sweet person" and a "doting father." He "ran the family," doing all of the cooking – something he enjoys, especially baking. He also does the laundry, grocery shopping, and general housekeeping. That is one of Iz's attributes that she most admires: his responsibility. It is right up there with his sense of humor and intelligence. One of his mannerisms that she loves about him, one he is not even consciously aware of doing, is how he puckers his lips out "like duck lips" whenever he is concentrating intently on something.

Tammie turns into a "pampered princess" with Iz. She sleeps every day until about 7:00 a.m., while Iz wakes up by 6:30 to get Sarah fed and dressed, and then takes her to day care. He also picks Sarah up from day care after work.

On November 13, 2002, Iz's father dies suddenly, and Iz flies to Maine for the funeral. He had always wanted to try to reconcile with his dad, but his father's abrupt death prevents it.

In mid-December, Tammie and Iz go on a weekend getaway to the Quinault Beach Resort in Ocean Shores, Washington, to celebrate the two-year anniversary of when they first met. On the way there, they stop in Port Angeles to do some Christmas shopping. During the shop-

ping excursion, Tammie sneaks off and buys something without Iz's knowledge. When they arrive in Ocean Shores, they check into their room and unpack. Tammie hides her secret purchase inside a pair of slippers that she is also giving Iz. When he opens the box of slippers, he finds an engagement ring.

"What do you think," Tammie asks as he stares at the ring, "do you want to get married?"

Iz breaks into a broad smile and puts the ring on his finger.

"Yeah, let's do it!"

Tammie knew that he would accept the proposal. After all, he had mentioned getting married several times during the prior year. She simply wanted to beat him to the punch.

They celebrate all night long at the casino, and Tammie even convinces Iz to dance to an Al Green song on the casino's dance floor, the first time he has danced in public in his life. They decide that the same song, "Let's Stay Together," will be their wedding song and they plan a one-year timeline for the ceremony.

Fifteen

Using a Google Earth map as a reference, Keyes told the law enforcement team that on February 21, three weeks after killing Koenig, he had loaded his truck with her remains and driven approximately thirty-five miles north from Anchorage to Matanuska Lake, near the intersection of Parks Highway and Glenn Highway. He had considered hundreds of lakes when deciding on the best place to hide the body, and he originally wanted to use a bigger lake, but settled on Matanuska partly due to its depth, and also because of its proximity to Anchorage since he knew that he would need to make several trips to dispose of all of the body parts. He had given some thought to using the Knik River, but ultimately decided that Samantha's remains would be discovered too quickly there due to the approaching fishing season. Matanuska Lake attracted less fishermen since motorboats were not permitted on it.

He had no trouble parking in the lake's lot by Glen Highway. It was completely empty, just as he hoped it would be. He walked about five hundred yards out onto the lake's frozen surface, pulling a sled loaded with a forty-gallon tote bag filled with ice fishing equipment and other materials he had brought from home. When he found a suitable spot where he figured the lake would be deep enough, he unloaded some boards to build a wooden hut so that it would look like he was simply ice fishing.

He used a chain saw to cut a hole in the ice, but it took him longer than he anticipated because even though the ice was only about 20 inches thick – much thinner than the four or five feet it had been when he had ice fished in the past – the chain saw kept dying. After he cut an 8 x 8 foot square in the ice, he hit it with a heavy iron bar several times to break through to the water underneath.

He was the only person on the lake that day except for one other individual he could see ice fishing in the distance. The man seemed to be giving him a funny look, perhaps due to how long it had taken him to cut his "fishing" hole. Using a 100-foot length of twine with lead weights affixed at the end, he checked the depth of the water. The bottom of the lake was forty feet below, considerably shallower than the sixty or eighty feet he had anticipated, but he decided that it would be deep enough.

After about an hour, the hole cut and the ice shack fully built, he carefully took the shack apart in such a way that it could be easily reassembled. Then he covered the hole with a piece of plywood so it would not refreeze overnight. He did not want to risk doing anything more with the curious ice fisherman eyeballing him.

On his way back to the truck, he realized that he had missed a parent-teacher conference he was supposed to attend at his daughter's school. Since he had removed the battery from his cell phone before traveling to the lake, he had to drive to Eagle River for another one to call his daughter's teacher and reschedule the conference.

The next day, he returned to the lake with Samantha's head, legs, and arms. He had stuffed the body parts in plastic bags, using three bags for each part. Before bagging them, he had wrapped the parts with baling wire. Both arms were bound together into one bundle, but the head and legs were all in separate bags.

Keyes paused in his narrative and looked around the room.

"You're going to need five different bags to gather up her body," he told the investigators with a faint chuckle.

———————

Returning to his story, he recalled how he had debated bringing the entire body to the lake and being done with it in one day. However, he knew that he could not carry all of the body parts from his truck to the ice hole in one trip, and it would not have been safe to leave any parts in the truck unattended or risk being seen making multiple trips back and forth. After towing his cargo to the fishing hole, he quickly reassembled the ice fishing shack. Under cover of the shack, he removed Samantha's body parts from the bags. To make sure they sank, he attached several heavy fishing weights to each part before dropping it through the hole in the ice.

In less than ten minutes, all four of the bundled body parts had disappeared into the cold depths of the frozen lake. Satisfied that the parts had sunk to the bottom, he started a small fire, sat back, and fished. He was alone on the ice the entire time, enjoying the peace and quiet. Over the next four or five hours, he caught a few fish and then disassembled the fishing shack before departing around 2:00 p.m. He left in plenty of time to make the rescheduled parent-teacher conference at his daughter's school to discuss putting her into a gifted program. That night, he pan fried the fish he had caught, savoring a simple, home-cooked dinner.

The following day, he made one last trip to the lake, this time bringing Samantha's dismembered torso with him. He followed the same procedure for disposing of it that he had used the day before, but the torso was heavier than the other parts had been and he slipped when he dropped it into the hole. Still, it only took a few minutes for the torso to sink into the dark waters of the lake. Once again, having finished his grisly task, he sat down, relaxed, and fished. Four or five hours later, he disassembled the shack one final time. Then he filled the hole back up with ice and threw some snow around it to conceal the location.

Having disposed of Samantha Koenig's body, Keyes turned his attention to getting rid of the other evidence that could link him to her murder. First, after returning home, he burned most of the tools he had used in getting rid of the body. Then, on March 1, he towed a trailer carrying 460 pounds of items to the Anchorage Landfill. Among the things he discarded were the typewriter he had used to compose the ransom note and the newspaper used in the accompanying photo. As an additional precaution, before taking the typewriter to the landfill, he removed the ink cartridge and burned it in the fireplace at his home. He added the ashes to the load of items discarded at the landfill.

While Keyes recounted the details of his abduction and cold-blooded murder of Samantha Koenig, Kevin Feldis and the others in the room could not help but notice the level of excitement with which he told his story. It seemed as if he was actually reliving the events as he grew increasingly animated and excited. As Feldis listened, he became convinced that the Koenig case was not the first time that Keyes had killed someone.

"Did you save anything from Samantha?" Feldis asked, referring to the well-known habit of serial killers.

"Like a souvenir?" Keyes asked in reply.

"Uh-huh," Feldis confirmed.

"No," Keyes said flatly.

But he had already told the investigators more than they would have ever learned on their own, and he seemed eager to do so, apparently relishing the opportunity to relive the events.

Keyes gazed across the table at Doll.

"You got your monster," he said with a smile.

On April 2, Keyes briefly met with the team of investigators again. He greeted them like old friends as he entered the Anchorage Correctional Facility's interview room, and he soon expressed irritation with his court-appointed lawyer.

"My attorney and I are not on the same page," he said, mentioning that he wanted to move his case along as rapidly as possible, while the attorney wanted the opposite.

The investigators pressed him to talk about other killings, hinting that doing so might get him what he wanted more quickly.

"I'm happy to help," he said, "but it's got to be on my terms, and my terms are not unreasonable. I'm not in this for the glory. I'm not trying to get on TV. And I'm not a person who is going to be bullied. There's not anything you can threaten me with, or say to me, or take away from me, or give to me – except for what I want."

He seemed to be baiting the interviewers with the information that he could provide.

"Just a few words out of my mouth will save you thousands of man hours," he assured them.

Detective Doll asked if he wanted her to stay involved in the case.

"Yeah, I don't like crowds," he replied. "I don't do well in court. I don't do well in front of a lot of people. If it's just a few people I can talk to throughout this, then it's going to go faster. It's going to go easier. I don't want to talk to people from Quantico. I don't care who's in the other room, I don't care who's recording, I don't care who's listening, but for the face-to-face stuff . . ." his voice trailed off.

Sensing a connection with him, Doll tried to get him to talk about other murders, what they had previously referred to as "more chapters to this book."

"Think about your loved ones," she urged. "Wouldn't you want to know if they're never coming home?"

Keyes weighed her words before answering.

"I'll give it some thought," he told her. "I'll let you know what I decide."

That evening, divers from the FBI's Underwater Search and Evidence Response Team recovered Samantha Koenig's dismembered body from Matanuska Lake. FBI personnel used snow machines and ATVs to move back and forth between a staging area in the parking lot and the recovery site approximately 400 yards out on the frozen lake. Earlier that morning, they had used chain saws to cut a four- foot long triangular hole in the three-feet-thick ice, and then employed sonar and a remotely operated vehicle to search under the ice. Divers entered the dark, murky water around 7:30 p.m., still relying on sonar to guide them to Samantha's remains about forty feet beneath the frigid surface.

Keven Sturgeon, a resident of a house overlooking the lake, watched until investigators began packing up their equipment shortly before 9:00 p.m. Sturgeon had moved to Alaska from Los Angeles, hoping for a slower paced, more tranquil way of life, but he had been following the Koenig case in the news.

"I was wondering if they were ever going to find her," he said. "I pray for her family."

Reading from a prepared statement, Special Agent Mary Rook, head of the FBI's Anchorage division, briefed reporters about the recovery of the body, but then refused to answer any questions. She pointed out that the case had been particularly challenging for the FBI and APD because of the randomness of Samantha's selection as a victim.

"I believe it was largely the dissociative nature of this crime that so perplexed investigators," Rook said. "In fact, were it not for the efforts of several very alert and dedicated Texas law enforcement officers, Samantha's abductor might still be at large."

She acknowledged the public's frustration with the limited amount of information that law enforcement had released about the case, and she offered her condolences to Samantha Koenig's family.

"Although some questions have been answered today," Rook said, "I know those answers offer little consolation for the Koenig family and many questions remain."

The next morning, a shrine of flowers, Teddy bears, and candles appeared at the Common Grounds coffee stand where Samantha had been abducted. Many of those contributing to the shrine left notes.

I did not know this child, one man wrote, *but her passing breaks my heart. Clearly monsters live among us.*

Members of the FBI dive team, working with Anchorage
Police and Alaska State Troopers, search Matanuska
Lake in Anchorage for Samantha Koenig's body on
April 2, 2012. Keyes was indicted on April 18 in
connection with Koenig's murder. (FBI Files)

(Tammie & Iz - 2003)

Six months after Sarah's birth, doctors diagnose that Tammie has tumors in the lining of her uterus. To help alleviate chronic pain caused by her condition, the doctors prescribe her pain pills. Within months of diagnosis, she has to have a hysterectomy, and to make matters worse, she develops an addiction to the pain pills.

As Tammie's condition worsens, Iz becomes Sarah's primary caretaker. He wakes her up and dresses her every morning for day care, picking out clothes for her and braiding her hair. She becomes a "daddy's girl" as Iz assumes more and more of the responsibilities of raising her.

Tammie often disagrees with Iz about parenting styles and how best to discipline their daughter. He tends to be stricter than Tammie – too strict she often thinks – while she prefers to be more liberal with rules and more lax with punishments. Despite Iz's greater parenting role, or perhaps in some ways because of it, his drinking steadily increases.

Along with his new role as a father, Iz has a new job with the Makah Tribe's Parks and Recreation Department, running a one-man beautification project in a newly formed position picking up litter and building trails, restrooms, and even a farmer's market. Although the job had been posted and he applied for it like anyone else, his hiring generates considerable controversy, at least initially, because he is not a Native. However, the tribal community welcomes him when they see how hard he worked and how well he did the job. It is a forty-hour-a-week job, 8 AM to 5 PM, starting at $13 an hour, a rate that is up to $20 an hour by the time he leaves five years later. He enjoys the work and excels at it, and he is well-liked throughout the community.

Sixteen

With Samantha Koenig's killer identified and securely in custody, investigators began to piece together details about his background.

Keyes came into the world on a cold winter's day on January 7, 1978, in Richmond, Utah, a small town of 2,000 people located about one hundred miles north-east of Salt Lake City. His parents, Heidi Hakansson and John Jeffery Keyes, a self-described "maintenance man," had married three years earlier. Fundamentalist Christians, they named many of their children based on the Bible, godly traits, or nature, choosing such names as Isaac, Charity, Hosanna, and Sunshine. For their first son, they decided on the name, "Israel," a Hebrew name meaning, "Who prevails with God," or "He who struggles with God." It was the same name given to Jacob in the Old Testament after he wrestled with God's angel. And during the course of his life, Israel Keyes would have his own struggles with God.

While still a boy, Keyes moved with his family to Colville, Washington, a small town of less than 5,000 inhabitants in Stevens County. During much of his formative years, he lived on Rocky Creek Road in a small cabin with a wood-heated stove and no electricity. He was homeschooled and exposed to the white supremacist beliefs of the

Christian Identity movement through a church located near the Canadian border called The Ark. His friends and neighbors included Chevie and Cheyne Kehoe, who lived about a half-mile from him off Aladdin Road north of town. Of the nine Keyes children, five girls and four boys, Israel was the second oldest and the eldest son.

Keyes found that he had a natural talent for carpentry work, an occupation made nobler by Christ's identification as a carpenter prior to pursuing his ministry. He built his first wood cabin when he was sixteen and worked for a general contractor in Colville between 1995 and 1997.

In the late 1990s, the Keyes family moved to a mostly Amish community in Smyrna, Maine, where they dabbled in the production of maple syrup, tapping trees and collecting the sweet sap. The family attended Amish services for a few years, but never fully joined the Amish community. As a friend of the family described it, Keyes's mother "changed religions like musical chairs." She came across as "very creepy" and "cult minded," and seemed to be running a "religious merry-go-round." She eventually lost interest in the Amish ways of life just as she had briefly dabbled in Mormonism before moving to Maine. Due to their mother's oppressive religious views, the Keyes children had to sneak over to a friend's house if they wanted to watch a movie, even a western like Clint Eastwood's *A Fistful of Dollars*, and they were not allowed to play musical instruments because their mother believed that doing so "was against God."

Israel was the "prince of the family," and all of his siblings looked up to him. However, when he was about seventeen, he had a falling out with his parents, rejecting their religious faith, and in an early manifestation of his struggles with God, declaring himself to be an Atheist. As a result of this rebellious (and in the eyes of his overbearing mother) blasphemous act, he was kicked out of the family home, and his parents instructed his brothers and sisters that they could not have any contact with him.

On July 9, 1998, estranged from his family, Keyes travelled to New Jersey and enlisted in the United States Army. He served as a Specialist in Alpha Company, 1st Battalion, 5th Infantry, stationed at Fort Lewis near Tacoma, Washington, and at Fort Hood in Texas. While in the Army, he also spent some time in Sinai, Egypt. While stationed in Egypt, Keyes shared a barracks with Sean McGuire, and the two formed a friendship. However, McGuire never fully dropped his guard around Keyes, who when once offended by something McGuire had said, told him – in what McGuire deemed to be all seriousness – "I want to kill you, McGuire."

While he was in the Army, Keyes manned mortars, handled automatic weapons, and located and neutralized land mines. In February 2001, while still stationed at Fort Lewis, he was arrested for driving under the influence, and pursuant to a plea agreement, he received a one-day jail sentence and a $350 fine. Keyes was awarded an Army Achievement Medal for "meritorious service while assigned as a gunner and assistant gunner from the second of December 1998 to the eighth of July, 2001 in the Alpha Company 60mm mortar section."

He later told investigators that in 1997 or 1998, prior to his enlistment in the Army, he raped a young, teenaged girl – he guessed she was between 14 or 18 years old – who was tubing down the Deschutes River near Maupin, Oregon. He had stalked the unknown girl as she floated down the river with friends. Hidden in the tree line, he waited patiently for an opportunity to strike. When the girl became separated from her group, he dragged her into the woods and "very violently sexually assaulted her." He had originally intended to kill her, but instead put her back in her inner tube and allowed her to float away.

Shortly before being honorably discharged from the Army in 2001, Keyes met Tammie Hawkins, and when she moved back to Neah Bay, Keyes moved in with her. At the time of his discharge from the Army and relocation to Neah Bay, Keyes stood a muscular six feet two inches in height. He could be quiet and reserved when around people he did not know, but he was animated, outgoing, and personable when with friends. He liked heavy metal music and violent movies, often driving around with songs from Lacuna Coil or Megadeth blaring from his truck's speakers, but he also enjoyed more mainstream music like Ace of Base.

In Neah Bay, Keyes took a job with the Makah Tribal Council in its new Parks and Recreation Department, building trails and recreational buildings, and doing various construction projects on the side for customers on the weekends. On his construction company's website, Keyes described his job duties while at Neah Bay:

> Built many trails, recreational buildings, and assisted the public works department in times of need or emergency situations. Coordinated the purchase, maintenance, and operation of machinery and equipment including a pump truck and portable as well as permanent remote toilet facilities. Neah Bay is a very small village and my position with the Tribe and the projects that I completed for them gave me an excellent reputation with the locals. This allowed me a unique opportunity to do a wide variety of construction projects for many customers on weekends.

He "fit right in" on the reservation and got along well with his coworkers, often joining them in playing practical jokes on one another. He was just as often the victim as the prankster. A co-worker recalled the time all of the tires on Keyes's truck were flattened, but made to look normal by putting blocks under the truck. When he tried to drive away after work with his usual pedal-to-the-metal acceleration, the truck barely budged as it collapsed onto the flat tires. Those living in the small, tight-knit community considered him to be pleasant, respectful, and always helpful. It seemed that he was always volunteering to help others. His carpentry work in the form of beautification benches for the community, ramps for the elderly, or additions to houses was "admired by everyone."

Around this time, he murdered an unknown couple in Washington, burying them in an unidentified valley. In the summer or fall of 2005 or 2006, he murdered two more unknown victims, disposing of one of the bodies in Lake Crescent in Washington State. All the while, he enjoyed living a double life, harboring his dark secrets, protecting them from even his closest friends.

Keyes Construction Website Photo

Photo Keyes had on his website

(Tammie & Iz - 2003 – Northwest Washington)

Shortly after 9:00 p.m., nineteen-year-old Wendy Morris drives down a dark, empty road. State Route 112 spans some sixty-one miles, passing through the heart of the Olympic Peninsula between the Makah Indian Reservation to the west and Highway 101 to the east. It can be a lonely haul in this remote part of northeastern Washington, especially at night, but it is a drive that Wendy has made many times before, so the inevitable sense of isolation no longer bothers her. Her music keeps her company. Whenever a feeling of loneliness creeps in, she cranks up the stereo system in her Honda Civic and lets the music be a reassuring companion.

As Wendy gazes ahead into the darkness, something in the dashboard catches her eye. She frowns when she sees that the low fuel warning light has come on, bathing the black cabin of her car in an ominous yellow glow. She shudders at the thought of running out of gas, at night, alone, on such an isolated stretch of road. She knows from past experience that gas stations are few and far between in the area, but she is reasonably confident that there will be one a few miles up the road.

Fortune seems to favor her when the station comes into view in the distance. She manages a slight smile, happy to have her recollection proved correct, but more relieved to know that she will not be breaking down in the middle of nowhere.

She turns into the station and pulls up beside a gas pump. The attendant has long since gone home, but the pump's self-service credit card readers are still operating. As the dispenser click-clacks to the rhythm of the gallons pumped display, Wendy glances around the station. It is virtually deserted. Not a vehicle is in sight except for one pick-up truck backed into a spot on the far side of the parking lot. Looking closer, she can see the outline of a dark figure sitting behind the steering wheel of the truck. A chill runs down her spine when she realizes that the figure is watching her, its unseen eyes fixated on her as she finishes pumping the gas and takes her receipt from the fuel dispenser.

Unnerved by the unknown watcher, Wendy's relief at having found the gas station rapidly gives way to fear. Steadying herself, she starts the Civic's engine and nervously pulls away from the gas pump, all the while keeping a wary eye on the figure in the truck. She turns back onto the road and quickly accelerates, resuming her journey east, silently breathing a sigh of relief as the gas station recedes in the rear-view mirror.

Then the truck turns onto the road after her.

Wendy's heart begins to race as she watches the truck growing larger in her rear-view mirror. She speeds up, but the truck keeps pace behind her. It draws so close that when she looks in the mirror again, the truck's headlights are barely visible, almost fully obscured by their proximity to her rear bumper. She watches with mounting alarm as the truck accelerates again and passes her. For a moment, she thinks that it will keep going, but then it darts back into the lane in front of her and screeches to a halt.

As Wendy slams on her brakes to avoid a collision, the force of the sudden stop jars her violently forward in her seat. The truck sits motionless in front of her, quietly idling as its brake lights illuminate an area of asphalt in eerie, blood-red light.

Wendy stares in panicked disbelief at her useless cell phone, its battery long-since dead. She curses herself for not charging it before starting the trip, though she knows that getting a signal in such a secluded area is unlikely anyway.

After regaining her composure, she realizes that she needs to get away from the truck as quickly as possible. She presses down on the gas pedal and pulls into the opposite lane, passing to the left of the truck, but she goes no more than twenty feet before it races after her again. A surreal, but frightening cat-and-mouse pursuit ensues for nearly an hour.

After yet another traumatic cut-off and sudden, perilous stop, Wendy's eyes widen in terror as the driver's side door of the truck flies open and the dark figure behind the wheel reveals itself. In the dull, yellow beams of her headlights, the shadowy frame of a man steps out from the door and turns around to face her. Clad in black jeans and a t-shirt with the arms cut out, the man looks to be in his twenties. Thin, but muscular, he stands well over six feet tall.

With an unnerving grin, the man gestures for Wendy to come over to him, silently beckoning her forward with his hands. Wendy's heart gallops in her chest, the adrenaline surge pushing her fully into fight-or-flight mode. Whatever her pursuer wants, she knows that it cannot be good. Taking a deep breath, she musters the courage to steer past him, answering his look of angry surprise with a nervous half-smile as she goes by.

Her spirits sink as she watches the man jump back into his truck and speed after her once more. She starts to panic, imagining the truck ramming into her, running her off the road. She sees herself knocked senseless as she crashes, and she imagines the man's fearful grin as he grabs her from the car.

But then they approach a more populated area near the junction of Highway 101. The truck slows down behind her, drifting steadily back until it stops and turns around. Wendy watches in disbelief as the truck recedes into the distance. For the first time in over an hour, she begins to relax.

Behind her in the distance, the truck's taillights slowly fade away as it heads west, back toward Neah Bay, blending into the darkness in search of new prey.

Seventeen

J ames Koenig would never forget the call he received from the FBI informing him that Samantha's remains had been recovered. Although he knew that there was little chance of finding her alive, James was still devastated by the news of his daughter's death.

"That part of me is gone," he said later. "It was devastating. My heart's gone. Having her back home with me is better than not ever knowing where she's at, so there's a little comfort in that. But I don't think I'll ever have closure on this."

Samantha's aunt, Pamela Garner, posted an online message thanking members of the community for their outpouring of support while Samantha was missing. *I know that she will be sharing her infectious laughter, bubbly personality, kind heart, corky [sic] quick wit, and her amazing soul with everyone above and will be with us forever in spirit and looking down on us,* Garner wrote.

After the lynch-mob mentality they were subjected to by many in the Anchorage community, Chris Bird and his mother decided that they had had enough. They were leaving town, driving separate cars in a convoy through Canada on their way back to North Carolina, when Chris's cell phone rang. He had to pull over and pull himself together when he heard the news that Samantha's remains had been found.

During a brief meeting on April 5 at the Anchorage Correctional Complex, Keyes expressed his frustration that he had not been able to fire his attorney. He told Doll and Bell that he wanted to speak to federal prosecutors before providing any more information about his crimes.

Fearing the loss of whatever bond may have existed between them, Doll slipped Keyes a piece of paper with her name and phone number on it.

"I really don't do this very often," she said in a slightly embarrassed tone, a hint of flirtation evident in her voice.

"That's okay," Keyes smiled jokingly in reply. "I don't get numbers in jail very often."

A few days before Easter, James Koenig posted a message on the "Help Find Samantha Koenig" Facebook page announcing that the family would be having Samantha's remains cremated at sunrise on April 8, Easter morning. He wrote that Easter would be an appropriate day for Samantha's cremation "because of the angel that she is."

Around 7:45 p.m. on April 6, George Murtie and his wife, Linda, were getting ready to eat dinner at their home in Essex. For Murtie, it had been another long, frustrating day of working the Currier case.

"You know, I don't think we're ever going to solve this case," Murtie told her with a depressed sigh. "I feel so bad for the Currier family," he said, nearly tearing up as he thought about the anguish they had been going through.

Because of the lack of physical evidence in the case, he had been forced to rely largely on leads and tips, and the investigation had been a roller coaster ride of emotions continually chasing down dead-end leads that never panned out. He felt like a hamster on a wheel, enthusiastically pursuing leads to the point of exhaustion, but ultimately going nowhere. Knowing that he was not any closer to the truth of what happened despite all of the hours he had spent working the case was immensely discouraging, and it depressed him to think that he might never find out what happened to Bill and Lorraine. Most difficult of all was having to contact the Currier family members each week and telling them that he had nothing new to report about the location or status of their missing loved ones.

Linda knew that not being able to solve the case or bring any type of closure to the Currier family was tearing George up inside. Indeed, that compassion and concern for others was one of the things she most loved about him.

"I'm sure something will turn up on it," she assured him, joining him at the table.

They ate and talked about their day's events.

Fifteen minutes later, the phone rang. George answered to find Michelle Delpha from the FBI on the other end of the line. She had news to share. State and federal authorities in Anchorage, Alaska, had a male suspect in custody for an abduction and murder that occurred there. The suspect had been arrested in mid-March, and he had recently confessed to killing Bill and Lorraine Currier as well.

George was nearly too stunned to speak. It was, Linda would later say, a moment of divine intervention.

During the ensuing phone discussion, George learned that Keyes mentioned two possible locations for an abandoned farmhouse where he had murdered the Curriers and left their bodies. After hanging up, George quickly dressed to go check out the sites. Just as he was heading out the door, the phone rang again. This time it was his pregnant daughter calling. Her water had broken and she was on her way to the hospital to deliver George's second grandchild. Although his heart dearly wanted to speed to the hospital to be there for the birth of his grandchild, George's sense of duty, and his desire to help the Currier family find their loved ones, compelled him to go investigate the possible locations of Bill and Lorraine's bodies. As he kissed Linda goodbye, she wrapped her arms around him for a long embrace, then he stepped out the door.

Earlier that day in Anchorage, Keyes had sat for another interview in the U.S. Attorney's Office with the usual team of investigators. During an hour-and-a-half meeting, the investigators confronted Keyes with evidence recovered from his home computer relevant to the disappearance of Bill and Lorraine Currier. Sporting a slight grin, Keyes reminded them how fortuitous his arrest had been.

"Frankly," he told them, "If I hadn't been picked up in Texas, that computer would be in a landfill right now because on March 24, I was going to get Kimberly a new one."

U.S. Attorney Kevin Feldis pressed him to disclose one of his other killings.

"Give me a body," Feldis suggested, "Give me something to work with so I can move forward."

But Keyes was not ready to go all-in.

"I'm not going to play all of my cards," he responded slyly.

"Keep most of your cards," Feldis replied. "Give me something that I'm going to find eventually anyway."

Keyes had another agenda; however, he wanted to discuss his motivations for continuing to talk with the investigators, and he wanted assurances from them that his goals could be met. His primary reason for talking with investigators was that he wanted the "inevitable" – the death penalty – within one year.

"The reason I'm doing this is that I know, I always knew, that I was playing for keeps, and I knew that this was inevitable. What's going to happen is going to happen. I accept that. And I am ready for it. I'm more than ready for it," he stressed. "My issue is how long it's taking. And how long it could take if we don't figure out a way to expedite things."

After some further prodding by Feldis, Keyes elaborated on his wish to expedite the process.

"I want an execution date. I want this whole thing wrapped up and over with as soon as possible. I want this whole thing done in a year. From today, start to finish. I'll plead guilty to whatever. I'll give you every single gory detail you want – but that's what I want."

His other motivation sprang from the desire to shield his daughter, as much as possible, from what he had done.

"I want my kid to have a chance to grow up. She's in a safe place and she's not going to have to see any of this. I want her to have a chance to grow up and not have all of this hanging over her head."

Feldis and the others assured him that if he would plead guilty to the Koenig murder, they would work with him to make sure that certain aspects of the crime would not be made public. Keyes thought carefully for a few minutes before responding.

"All right, I'll give you two bodies, and a name," he sighed reluctantly. "But that's all I'll give you today. The two bodies. And a name. If I get a cigar," he said with a laugh. He also told them that he would need a computer screen and access to Google Maps. They asked him what area of the country the map should include.

"Burlington, Vermont," he coolly replied.

After being provided access to Googlemap, he pointed out the pertinent locations of the crime and revealed two names: Bill and Lorraine

Currier. As in the Koenig case, Feldis wanted to understand how Keyes had selected his victims.

"How'd you meet them?" he asked.

"I *didn't* meet them," Keyes replied.

"Well, how'd you run into them?"

"I didn't," he said pointedly.

"So why'd you pick these folks?"

Keyes looked at him with an agitated expression, his brow furrowed in annoyance that his interrogator could not understand the simple reality of the situation.

"I didn't," he explained. "It was just random."

Feldis showed him a photograph of the Curriers that the Essex Police had used on missing persons posters. Keyes glanced at the photo and confirmed that the man and woman smiling at the camera were the people that he had killed.

"They're in big black trash bags," Keyes added in passing. "Probably skeletal by now."

Keyes yawned at times as he described the location of the Curriers' house, the Handy Suites hotel where he had stayed at the time of the killing, and his preparations for the crime, including the difficulty he had encountered in finding trash bags large enough for the job. His plan had been to fly from Anchorage to Chicago – on Alaskan Airlines, his preferred air carrier – drive to Indiana to see family, drive to New York to check on the property he owned there, then go to Vermont, New Hampshire, and Maine. He purchased a fishing license in Vermont, fished for a couple of days while staying at the Handy Suites hotel, and then, on the final night he was planning on being in Vermont, he abducted and killed the Curriers.

He had driven around the Essex area several days prior, looking at churches and unoccupied houses as potential execution sites for whoever he abducted. He stumbled across the site he ended up selecting, an abandoned farmhouse that he had "just happened to see" on his way back to Burlington. The old farmhouse had a For Sale sign out front.

"That's why I picked it," he said. "I could tell it was not a hot property. It was pretty much run down and unlivable inside. Right across the street from the house, which I thought was kind of funny at the time, there was a sheriff's car."

He explained that he originally planned on trying to get ransom money by using the Curriers' cell phones to text their employers and family – a plan similar to the one that he later used in the Samantha Koenig case – but one of the Curriers' cell phones only worked for emergency calls and the other did not have the ability to send texts. He had taken the Curriers' ATM card and even scratched their PIN on the front of it, but then never further pursued the matter.

"It was obvious they didn't have a lot of money," he pointed out. "They told me that they only had $100 in their account."

Although he had given them some information about the Currier murders, Keyes seemed to enjoy teasing the investigators about the information that he was *not* giving them.

"I'm not going to give you much more in that case until I have my date," he said with a laugh. "There's other things you're probably not going to find out about me unless I talk about them, and I probably won't talk about them. I'll probably just let sleeping dogs lie so to speak."

Before they ended for the day, he reiterated his underlying motivation in talking to them.

"My ultimate goal here is to keep this as quick and clean, over and done with, as possible. My only concern is that not every detail comes out as to my motivations and what actually happened. I'd rather that stuff not *ever* come out, at least not until I'm not around anymore," he said with a disturbing chuckle.

On Saturday, April 7, James Koenig posted on the Facebook page, "Please Help Find Samantha Koenig," part of a letter that he had written to his deceased daughter:

Samantha, I knew from the first day we laid eyes on one another that we were destined to hold each other's hearts within our own. . . I am so proud to have been a part of watching you blossom into the beautiful young lady you are, and am so sorry I wasn't there to protect you. I know that everything happens for a reason, but that is a burden that will weigh heavily on my heart for a very long time. . . Please fly with the angels and may you rest in peace baby girl. Love, Daddy

Four thousand miles away in Vermont, George Murtie learned that during Israel Keyes's confession to killing Bill and Lorraine Currier, he had mentioned staying at a hotel within walking distance of the Curriers' home. Since the closest hotel to the crime scene was the Handy Suites hotel on Susie Wilson Road, Murtie directed his investigators to check whether Keyes had ever stayed there. A quick review of hotel records confirmed that Keyes had stayed there June 7 through June 9, 2012, as well as in April of 2009.

———————

At daybreak on April 8, Easter Sunday, James Koenig and other family members gathered for the cremation of Samantha's remains, and then went outside to watch the sunrise.

———————

Later that day, Duane Tortolani posted a final goodbye to his departed girlfriend.

Samantha Koenig, love of my life, I will never forget you and I will love you till the day I die and am able to come be with you again. I'll see you in a little bit baby. Always and forever.

———————

The next day, April 9, Murtie continued his investigation into what had happened to the abandoned farmhouse at 32 Upper Main Street, the site he confirmed as the location where Keyes had killed the Curriers. An interview with an excavator operator at the demolition company that had demolished the farmhouse revealed that the debris had been trucked away to a landfill in Coventry, Vermont.

The employee recalled noticing a horrible smell "like a dead animal" emanating from the basement when the excavator punched through the floor level of the building, but he did not venture down into the basement to investigate the source of the stench. He also remembered seeing a large trash bag being extracted from the southeast corner of the cellar. He had used the excavator's bucket to reach into the basement hole and drag the contents toward him against one of its walls. The excavator then lifted the contents out bucketful by bucketful, dropping the debris into a dump truck while any metal was sorted out and set aside. The company's records revealed that the dump truck took a total of eight loads of debris to the Williston transfer station, where it would have subsequently been taken to the Coventry landfill.

Dave Gauthier, a property caretaker for the owner of the 32 Upper Main Street property, inspected the site just before the demolition. He recalled noticing a burned area where it appeared that someone had tried to start a fire, but he had avoided going into the basement because it "smelled too bad." Although his role of property supervisor often put him in contact with the installation and cleaning of septic systems, the "powerful stench" emanating from the basement at 32 Upper Main Street limited his investigation to opening the door at the top of the stairway and shining his flashlight down into the darkness. He remembered seeing a couple of garbage bags on the floor, but he assumed they simply contained common household trash.

At 11:00 a.m., an investigative team with representatives from the Essex Police Department, FBI, and Vermont State Police met to discuss the status of the Currier case. During the meeting, the FBI assured Murtie and his colleagues that the case would not become a federal investigation, but that the FBI would work with local law enforcement in trying to find the Curriers. The group had a lengthy discussion about forming a media strategy for the case, an important issue in light of the fact that Keyes had made it clear that he would stop cooperating with investigators if his name came out in media reports. Murtie urged everyone at the meeting to "work with the utmost caution" to ensure that Keyes's identity be kept secret, and all in attendance acknowledged that getting as much information as possible from Keyes about his 14-year killing career should be a top priority. They agreed that, when dealing with the media, they should be vague about the source of any information learned from Keyes in connection with the Currier case.

Murtie left the meeting in good spirits, relieved that, despite the FBI's suddenly increased involvement, his department would remain in charge of the Currier investigation. However, his relief would be short lived. Later in the day, he received a surprising phone call from Michelle Delpha. She informed him that the FBI was taking over the case and that Keyes's connection to the Curriers would now be investigated federally. Exasperated by the sudden shift of view, Murtie retorted that unless he heard otherwise from his captain, he still considered the Currier investigation to be an Essex Police Department case concerning crimes against the State of Vermont.

On April 10, FBI Agent Payne phoned Murtie to fill him in on the basic details of the Samantha Koenig case. During their 90-minute conversation, Payne told him that Keyes wanted to be executed as quickly as possible and that he had confessed to the Currier murders only after learning that he could not get the death penalty in Alaska for killing Koenig. Payne described Keyes as being "very intelligent," but a "loner" with "bizarre sexual appetites."

Despite his misgivings about the federal investigators' role in the Currier case, Murtie prayed that playing Keyes's game would bring some relief to the families of his other missing victims.

Excavating site at 32 Upper Main Street (Essex Police)

Although Iz is doing well at work, things are beginning to fall apart with his relationship with Tammie. Her pain pill addiction has become a full-fledged opiate addiction, and he has started to withdraw, increasingly spending time on internet chat rooms as they both neglect their relationship. She notices that he is becoming "cold and quiet," but she is so strung out on opiates that she cannot comprehend the extent to which their relationship has deteriorated. Iz starts sleeping on the couch as they drift further apart. He tries to break up with her in the summer of 2004, but she is in denial. When she refuses to move out of the house, Iz moves out with Sarah. He fixes up a house downtown and falls into a short affair with another member of the Makah tribe.

After dating a couple of girls in Neah Bay, Iz meets someone new on the online dating site, match.com: 41-year-old Kimberly Anderson, a nurse practitioner living in Port Angeles.

Meanwhile, Tammie's addiction continues unabated until she is involved in a serious car accident. Due to her inebriation at the time of the accident, she serves 25 days in jail in Neah Bay followed by seven weeks of mandatory treatment at a drug rehabilitation facility. After completing her rehab stint, Tammie begins seeing Iz again, under the guise of visiting Sarah. She and Iz become sexually involved again, a situation that continues off and on for the rest of the time he remains in Neah Bay. But while Tammie wants to get back together as a couple, Iz is not willing. Her drug addiction has done too much damage.

The two still talk openly with each other, including Iz telling her about his relationship with Kimberly. He tells Tammie that he is attracted to Kimberly because of her intelligence and independence, similar traits that had attracted him to Tammie. On the night of Sarah's birthday, Iz tells Tammie that he has made plans to go to Port Angeles to see Kimberly. When he asks Tammie if she thinks that he should go, she tells him to do what he feels he needs to do. So he goes.

While Tammie tries to act unaffected by Iz's relationship with

Kimberly, inside it is eating at her. Increasingly consumed by jealousy, she leaves a note on Kim's gold Accord in the parking lot of the Clinicare where she works in downtown Port Angeles. The note discloses that Iz and Tammie are still seeing each other.

Despite Tammie's attempt at sabotaging Iz's new relationship, when Kimberly lands a new job in Alaska, she invites him to move there with her. Since Sarah is involved, he has to file a relocation request with the court to take her with him, and Tammie opposes it. She thinks that doing so will make him change his mind about moving.

As expected, the court denies the relocation request, and a heated custody battle ensues. Eventually, Iz relents and agrees to give custody of Sarah to Tammie, an act that shocks her. After realizing that he is moving to Alaska no matter what, Tammie agrees to share custody with him under an arrangement in which they will alternate which parent Sarah will live with on a yearly basis.

On March 1, 2007, Keyes departs Washington, drives through Canada on the Alaska-Canadian Highway, and arrives in Anchorage on March 9. He starts his own business, Keyes Construction, and over the next few years builds up a steady clientele based largely on the referrals and recommendations of customers for whom he completes construction projects.

On the internet site for his construction business, Keyes Construction, Keyes advertises Foundations to Finish work. Inside or out. I have the specialty tools and over ten years' experience to get the job done right! Advertising service for Anchorage and the "surrounding area," the website quotes hourly rates between $35 and $40 an hour for projects such as cedar fences, wood decks, bathrooms, and kitchen remodeling. A webpage providing his work history includes his three years of service in the Army and six years working for the Makah Tribal Council in Neah Bay. Several photos of finished projects adorn the site, including one of a smiling Keyes wearing his tool belt, proudly standing in front of a wooden stairway addition to the outside of a home.

Keyes and Kimberly Anderson move into an almost 2,000 square foot, three-bedroom, two-and-a-half bath home at 2456 Spurr Lane in the Turnagain neighborhood of Anchorage. Although the house had been constructed in 1971, Keyes puts his carpentry skills to work, remodeling and installing new lighting, plumbing, windows, French doors, and tile. He also adds a 120-square-foot frame storage shed at the end of the driveway beside the house.

Eighteen

Shortly after 9:00 a.m. on April 12, Essex police, accompanied by a Vermont State Police evidence recovery team, as well as FBI evidence recovery personnel, began searching the site where an abandoned farmhouse had previously stood at 32 Upper Main Street just over three miles from Bill and Lorraine Currier's house. The site, located across from the Morris State Farm Insurance office near Lang Farm, was now just a vacant lot.

Nearly twenty law enforcement personnel participated in the search, clad head-to-toe in white coveralls as they brandished rakes and shovels, occasionally sifting through various debris where the vacant, two-story stone and wood farmhouse had been demolished the previous fall. As a backhoe dug into the ground, two cadaver dogs paced around the area, periodically sniffing piles of soil being left by the backhoe.

The investigative team divided the search area into four quadrants, with two teams of evidence technicians searching two of the quadrants at a time. They recorded GPS coordinates at each corner of the quadrants as well as each location where potential evidence was recovered.

The backhoe operator placed material from the hole where the house's basement had been in a mechanized topsoil processor box, which separated rock, wood, and other large debris from the soil. Then investigators searched the processed soil by hand, pulling aside any remarkable objects. The search efforts ended at about 7:30 p.m., after which George Murtie received a call from his captain, conveying the unwelcome news that the FBI would be taking custody of all evidence at the end of each day.

A persistent wind blew through the site as the search resumed at 8:00 a.m. the next morning. A slightly smaller crew of twelve law enforcement personnel and one cadaver dog continued the search hoping to find something relevant to the case. Although the wind made it difficult to pinpoint the exact location, Murtie noticed an intermittent "odor of decomposition" coming from the general area where the basement had been. Afterward, a cadaver dog hit on a section of the southeast corner of the basement wall. The search concluded at 4:15 p.m. while the backhoe finished refilling the excavated hole where the farmhouse had once stood. Law enforcement personnel shared little information about the results of the search, other than to acknowledge that it related to the Currier investigation.

———

As the excavation ground to a close, worried residents of the Curriers' neighborhood continued to wonder what had happened to them.

"It's a little unsettling sitting on my living room couch every night and looking across the street to their house," said neighbor Pat Goddard. She was hopeful that the new search efforts would lead to some answers in the case. "At least it would bring some kind of closure to what happened to them and where they are located. But there are still a lot of unanswered questions as to why and how and who."

———

Later that evening, Agent Payne notified Murtie that a reporter from a CBS network in Vermont had contacted the Anchorage Police Department asking whether a connection existed between Israel Keyes and the Currier case.

———————

As Vermont authorities searched the site of the Currier murders, Keyes sat down again with his usual entourage of interviewers, this time for nearly two-and-a-half hours at the Anchorage Correctional Complex. Although they brought him a cigar and coffee, Keyes was not in good spirits. He made no secret of his annoyance over what he perceived to be a lack of progress in pursuing death penalty proceedings.

"It's been a one-way street so far except for the coffee and cigars," he told the interview team with obvious irritation.

"Death penalty cases take a lot of time," Feldis said, explaining that prosecutors had to follow the legal process to ensure that his rights were not violated.

Despite the explanation, Keyes could not understand why it was taking so long when, rather than fighting or trying to avoid it, he had expressly stated that he *wanted* the death penalty.

"I appreciate that you're concerned about my rights, but I'm not an ignorant person," Keyes replied.

"Why do you want the death penalty?" Feldis asked curiously.

Keyes answered without hesitation:

Because I want this all to be over. I don't want stuff hanging over my head while I sit in Supermax waiting for the next thing to come down the pipe.

As extreme as it might seem to some people, it really is not that extreme to me just because of my outlook on things. It's a personal opinion that I have of the way things are. And it's not going to change. And I knew, as soon as I started talking to you, I knew I was never getting out.

So for me, that is the death penalty. Because I'm not Bubba from the sticks who's sat in one town for all my life, and I can't be satisfied sitting in prison for all of my life. I've been lots of places, I've done lots of things, and sitting in prison for the rest of my life *is* the death penalty. To me, it's the same thing.

He looked at Feldis and smiled.

"I've never lived anywhere more than five or six years. I get bored easily, so you can see why sitting in jail waiting for this stuff to resolve is not really that attractive to me. I'd rather go out while I still have some sanity and good memories," he laughed.

He promised the investigators that he would give them all of the information they needed about his past – all the way back to his early teenaged years – if they would give him what he wanted. And he emphasized that they would never be able to learn the information he had on their own without his assistance.

"You're not going to find out much before I was in the Army," he said, "because, aside from having a driver's license, I wasn't on paper really. You're not going to find anyone in my past, with the exception of maybe one or two Army guys, who is going to have any suspicion whatsoever that I am the other person that I am. That's just the way it is," he said proudly. "This is going to be a shock to a lot of people."

He also assured them that the only evidence they would ever be able to find linking him to any murder was what they had already found on the computer when they seized it from his house, evidence which linked him solely to the Currier murders. Most of the evidence about his past crimes had been on his prior computer, the laptop he had used since living in Neah Bay, and that computer was long gone. He had disposed of it in an Anchorage landfill in November of 2011.

Feldis explained that they had to be careful about how they moved forward with any information he provided so that they could ensure that the information was properly controlled. Control was a notion the investigators raised repeatedly throughout the interview. It became the central theme around which they framed all of their discussions with Keyes.

"Do you want to control how this is released or do you want someone else to control it? You help us, and you get to keep control," Feldis reminded him.

Keyes was still not convinced of the need to move so slowly on his capital punishment case.

"If you're telling me that it's not going to happen in a year, then I'm losing interest in the whole thing," he warned. "I want to help you, but only if there's something in it for me. I don't feel any moral obligation to tell you anything. I don't want to give you any ancient history stuff," he chuckled. "I already know what you're going to be able to find and what you're not going to be able to find. I will share additional information, but only if I get what I want. Everybody in this room wants the same thing: you want me punished and I want to be punished."

Hoping to change the focus of the conversation, Feldis brought up something that Keyes had clearly not anticipated. Essex Police Department investigators had recently learned that the unoccupied farmhouse where Keyes hid the Curriers' bodies had subsequently been demolished.

"Guess I spoke too soon on that one," Keyes laughed with obvious surprise, a broad smile replacing his momentary look of astonishment. "I figured they'd be found pretty soon, but I didn't know it'd been demolished."

Feldis let the news sink in for a while, before getting Keyes to agree to reveal where he hid the gun that he used to kill Bill Currier, in exchange for another cigar and a bathroom break.

After the break, Keyes described how, on his way back to Vermont from Maine, he abandoned the ransom scheme he had originally planned, and he burned a suitcase containing the Curriers' belongings – including their cell phones, credit cards, and car keys – in a fire pit at a campsite in New Hampshire. He also confided that he had planned on burning the farmhouse in which he hid the Curriers' bodies, but because Bill Currier was such a large man, Keyes had trouble moving his body. By the time he finished hiding both of the bodies, it was 6:00 or 7:00 in the morning and the sun was coming up. It was too risky to burn the house in daylight, particularly since it had poured rain the night before and the wood would probably not burn very well.

The discussion then shifted to Keyes's crafty method of preparing for murders he planned on committing in the future. The method's centerpiece involved burying specifically chosen weapons, tools, and other items that he had assembled – he called them "kill-kits" -- at various locations around the country, including the one in which he stored the gun used in the Currier murders. He had used tool boxes for the first kill-kits, but he soon discovered that five-gallon plastic buckets worked better because they were more water resistant. He also mentioned that he had planned on burying the guns he had with him when he was arrested somewhere near the Grand Canyon north of Texas.

"Where'd you bury the other ones?" Russo asked, fishing for more information, but Keyes did not take the bait.

"If I tell you that, I'll never be able to use them again," he giggled in reply.

Then he remembered something he wanted to tell Detective Doll, a response to her attempts during a prior interview to persuade him to provide information about his other victims.

"I know you've talked about closure," he said, looking across the table at her. "Hypothetically speaking, if someone else is missing, would everybody rather just believe that they're missing, or think that something horribly terrible happened to them?" he asked rhetorically.

"The experts say that they're better off knowing," Feldis volunteered.

"I know I sure wouldn't want to know that," Keyes professed. "I'd feel better thinking they were off on a beach somewhere in Mexico than knowing they were horribly raped and murdered," he laughed, long and hard, as if he had just heard an irresistibly funny joke.

A few days later, on April 17, the United States Attorney's Office for Alaska filed a superseding grand jury indictment against Keyes in federal court. The indictment added two new counts against him: Kidnapping Resulting in Death (Count I), and Receipt and Possession of Ransom Money (Count II). The original charge from the initial indictment, Fraud with Access Device, remained as well, now renumbered as Count III.

After filing the indictment, federal and state authorities in Alaska emphasized their determination to see justice served. They intended to ensure that Keyes would receive a fitting punishment for his crime, whether it be life imprisonment or the death penalty.

"Our sympathies go out to Samantha's family," Kevin Feldis said. "It's important to her family and the community that justice will be done in this case. And now there's a judicial process under way."

Anchorage Police Chief Mark Mew expressed similar sentiments, stressing his department's resolve to do whatever it would take to provide justice for Samantha's family.

"We hoped to see her return safely, but this did not happen," Mew said. "You have my promise to leave no stone unturned in making sure that the person responsible for Samantha's death will be held accountable. The investigation into Israel Keyes and his criminal activities continues," he vowed.

———

At 12:30 p.m. the same day, Keyes sat for another interview at the U.S. Attorney's Office, this time with Bell, Goeden, Russo, and Feldis. He was in good humor from the get go, joking in response to Feldis's routine question as to whether he had any doubts about his competency.

"No, I'm more sane than most Americans," he said with a hearty laugh.

In response to Feldis's continuing push for information about other crimes, Keyes reiterated that he would not talk about anything he had done prior in time to the Currier murders.

"My concern about stuff that happened in the past is that the investigations of those things is going to drag stuff out longer. There is a history of this stuff. It goes back a long time," he said.

Following some additional prodding, he agreed to tell them about the arson and bank robbery that he had committed in Texas shortly before his arrest.

"But I want a cigar for it," he laughed.

Keyes recounted how he had travelled from Houston to New Orleans to go on a cruise, and then drove to Dallas after returning from the trip. He left Dallas early the next morning and then drove around small towns staking out a bank to rob.

"I was looking at banks . . . how many cameras there were around, where there was a good place to park the car, how many people were around, how close they were to the freeway, things like that."

Keyes told them that before traveling to a town to scope it out, he would usually research it on the internet. He looked for towns that had three or four routes out of town, then searched for the town's banks and police department so he could map out the area.

After finding a small-town bank that fit his criteria, he smoked a cigar in the parking lot, then casually walked in and robbed it. Immediately afterward, he stopped at a nearby gas station and filled up, watching the police cars responding to the robbery alarm as they raced by. Then he calmly drove back to the freeway and left the area.

He also revealed that he had been looking for churches in the area as potential sites to take someone to kill them.

"That's a personal thing," he explained in a sullen tone. "I have a lot of issues with organized religion. I'm sure it has something to do with the way I was raised but, for the most part, it's just my general outlook on the world and life in general."

His distaste for religion served as a central component of his moral outlook.

"It's fair to say that religion played a major part in how I ended up thinking and being the person I am. Religion had a lot to do with it – the way I was raised."

At one point during his Texas trip, he nearly abducted a woman who was walking a dog on a trail along a river. Although the dog was a large mastiff, he would not have had any problem shooting it. However, for some reason he could not explain, he decided not to do anything and just watched the unsuspecting woman as she walked away.

Keyes admitted that the arson and robbery had been "more spur of the moment" than what he typically undertook. He had been increasingly deviating from his usual pattern of taking his time in planning what to do next. He knew that the more impulsive behavior was inherently riskier, but it was also more exciting.

"I was kind of on an adrenaline phase," he explained, pointing out that the Koenig case had generated so much media coverage that he was "on a high" from all of the attention to the case and the lack of progress by law enforcement in identifying a suspect.

"That's always the reason I've done the kind of things I've done. Mostly for the adrenaline. It's not so much why I did it as 'why not?'"

And it had become increasingly difficult to control his urges. The craving to kill had been more and more in control of his actions in the years leading up to his arrest.

"I was kind of out of control," he explained. He felt an irresistible need to find another adrenaline rush, and the sense of calm that would normally return to him following one of his crimes diminished in duration every time. After killing Samantha Koenig, he "lost interest in work and whatever day-to-day stuff there was." He was increasingly compelled to seek out another high.

As the interview continued, Keyes briefly discussed his time in the Army, something he stressed that he had "wanted" to experience, in contrast to most of the other soldiers in the infantry who were there because they did not have any other options. His service in the military further shaped his philosophical and political views, and he recalled frequently getting into arguments with people posting on Al Jazeera's website.

"I have issues with the outlook most Americans have on the world and life in general," he remarked. "I take issue with U.S. foreign policy."

He also shared some details about his childhood, disclosing that he understood by the time he was 14-years old that he was "different" from other people, and that living two lives provided him a singular thrill.

"It was all like a mind game with me," he said. "That was all I needed. That was my adrenaline. That's where I got my kicks, I guess, being able to live two different lives and have no one have a clue."

He laughed as he explained the beginnings of his psychological dissonance.

I've known since I was 14 that there were things that I thought were normal and were ok[ay] that no one else seemed to think were normal and ok[ay]. So that's when I just started being a loner. I got in trouble a few times around that age. People found out about some of the stuff I did. Like my parents, and parents of other kids who would hang out with me. They would find out about some of the stuff I did. And that's when I just started doing stuff by myself pretty much exclusively.

There was one kid I grew up with and we used to break into houses together. But then there was a time I shot something – a dog or a cat – and that was too much for him. He couldn't handle it. And that was the last time I did stuff with him.

I had a lot of guns and I would always carry a gun. I used to carry a pistol all the time from the time I was about 14. By the time I was 14, I was basically the same size I am now. I didn't really look 14. And so I could get away with selling the guns I took from houses I broke into without anybody knowing about it.

One childhood incident that Keyes recounted particularly struck the investigators.

When I was 14 there were some of my parents' friends staying with us. There was a cat of ours that was always getting into the trash. It was my sister's. I told her "if that cat gets into the trash again I'm going to kill it."

And so there was a kid and one of his sisters and one of my sisters and we all went up into the woods and I had the cat with me. I took a piece of parachute cord and tied it to a tree. The cord was about ten feet long and I had a .22 revolver with me. And I shot the cat in the stomach and it ran around and around the tree, and then crashed into the tree and started vomiting.

And for me, I didn't really react. I actually kind of laughed a little because of the way it was running around the tree, but I looked at the kid who was my age and he was throwing up. Kind of traumatized I think. And he told his dad about it and, of course, his dad talked to my parents about it, and that was pretty much the last time anyone went into the woods with me. I learned my lesson from that.

Then he detailed how the Curriers came to be his Vermont victims.

When I first decided to do something in Vermont, I was looking at churches, because I had plans that whoever I was going to take was either going to end up in the church and leave them there for whoever went to that church that weekend to find, or I was going to burn the church with them in it.

Around eight or nine o'clock on the night of the murders, he prepared his guns and other abduction tools in his Handy Suites hotel room. He packed the .40 semi-automatic pistol, 10/22 handgun with silencer affixed, cable ties, duct tape, blindfolds, and other items in his backpack, then pulled on a rain jacket and headed out into the cold, wet night. After walking about a hundred feet down the street, he came to the Corner Stone Commons apartment complex and hid in the trees, watching and waiting for an appropriate victim. He wanted someone driving a decent car. He had already staked out three banks on Route 15 that he planned on robbing, and he needed a reliable car to use for the robberies.

After some time passed, a yellow Volkswagen entered the parking lot of the apartment complex and pulled into a spot near his hiding place. Seeing that a male driver was the lone occupant of the car, Keyes stepped out of the trees and began walking toward him. Before Keyes could reach him, the driver jumped out of the car, and clutching a newspaper over his head to fend off the rain, dashed to the front door of his apartment, quickly disappearing inside, leaving Keyes alone again in the downpour. Disappointed by this missed opportunity, Keyes returned to his hotel room and formed a new plan, deciding to abduct a male and female couple from a house, instead of carjacking a single male.

Around midnight, he left the Handy Suites again and walked less than a quarter of a mile to Colbert Street, scouting the neighborhood for a house that would meet his needs. One of his key criteria required that there be no children living at the home. This self-imposed condition had been a relatively recent rule.

"The one thing that I won't do is mess with kids," he told the investigators. "I never really thought that way until I had Sarah, until she was born. And then, after she was born, something kind of changed in the way I thought and I didn't want to do anything that would mess with kids."

After finding what looked to be a house that would fit the bill, Keyes removed a fan from the garage window and climbed inside the garage. The only car in the garage was unlocked, so he opened the glove box and read the car registration, happy to see that the owners of the house were an older couple. He scanned the garage for children's toys or sports equipment, but found nothing to suggest that any kids lived in the house.

He walked out through the garage door to survey the situation outside. A man at a neighboring house stepped outside leading a Golden Retriever on a leash. When the man stopped to light a cigarette, the dog began barking at Keyes, but after a few minutes, the neighbor finished his cigarette and took the dog into the house. Keyes waited several more minutes to make sure the man did not come back outside, and then he returned to the garage. He smashed in the window of a door leading to the kitchen and then mounted a "blitz" attack, completely surprising Bill and Lorraine Currier who were both sound asleep in their bed.

The next day, April 18, 2012, FBI agents conducted a search near the Blake Falls Reservoir off Raquette River Road in Parishville, New York. They recovered an orange, five-gallon, plastic Home Depot bucket hidden behind some rocks. The bucket contained components of a .22 Ruger, a silencer, ammunition, wires, and a flashlight. The "kill-kit" was the same one that Keyes had previously buried in the Winooski River nature area in Essex, Vermont, in 2009:

On April 9, 2009, wearing gloves, sunglasses, jeans, paste-on mustache, a goatee, and a Carhartt jacket with the hood pulled over his head, Keyes strolls into the Community Bank on Hosley Avenue in the small town of Tupper Lake, New York. He walks up to a bank teller, brandishes a silver Smith & Wesson .40 caliber handgun, demands money, and orders everyone in the bank to get on the floor. When he leaves, he walks out with approximately $10,000.

The next day, he checks into room 203 of the Handy Suites hotel on Susie Wilson Road in Essex, Vermont, paying $205 cash for a four-night stay. Later that day, he walks about a half-mile down a path at the Woodside Natural Area, commonly known as the 68 Acres. He picks out a spot of ground in a flat, wooded area along a bend in the Winooski River, and buries an orange, five-gallon, plastic Home Depot bucket containing an assortment of specifically chosen items, including the gun used in the Tupper Lake bank robbery.

On April 14, Keyes boards a commercial airline in Manchester, New Hampshire, bound for Alaska, the return flight on his round-trip ticket.

Even as he flies west, he looks forward to a return trip to Essex.

On April 19, 2012, Keyes appeared with his public defender in district court in Anchorage and pled not guilty to all three criminal charges against him.

The same day, at the other end of the country, George Murtie and his colleagues discussed a potential excavation of the Coventry landfill to try to find the bodies of Bill and Lorraine Currier. Since the estimated cost of the excavation exceeded $100,000, Murtie worried about whether it would be approved, particularly since the success rate for such searches was extremely low, no more than ten percent at best. Murtie understood the cost issue, but he hoped the operation would go forward. He dreaded having to tell Bill and Lorraine's families that their loved ones' bodies ended up in a garbage dump and, adding insult to injury, that they would have to stay there forever because investigators did not want to spend the money to recover them. His spirits were lifted when the recovery operation was finally approved.

Nineteen

On April 22, Samantha Koenig's family and friends were joined by other members of the Anchorage community at West High School to remember Samantha through a "Celebration of Life." A solemn procession of bikers, including The Dogs of the North and The Black Sheep, rode slowly through the city on their way to the ceremony. Many of those attending wore various shades of green, Samantha's favorite color. James Koenig wore a light green tie and a dark vest with a green peace symbol ribbon pinned to the left breast.

Ten large vases of floral arrangements decorated the stage, surrounding an angel statue standing prominently at the center. As a slide show of photographs from various stages of Samantha's life projected onto a large screen at the back of the stage, celebrants filled the West High School auditorium to its capacity.

The soft voices of a youth choir group began the ceremony as Steve Novakovich, owner of Legacy Funeral Homes, oversaw the event. Family friend Carl Sollenberger gave the opening prayer.

"Father, thank you so much for the time that we've had with Samantha. For blessing us with her beautiful smile, her loving heart, and her kind spirit. I pray for Sam's family and her friends, that You would comfort their hearts as only You can. And that you remind them, Lord, that Sam's not gone. Right now she lives on with You."

Sollenberger turned to address James Koenig, who sat stoically at the front of the auditorium.

"I'll never forget her beautiful smile," Sollenberger said respectfully. "That's how she always looked. Those memories, that's how I'm going to remember your daughter, and it's going to warm my heart for the rest of my life."

As Sollenberger walked quietly back to his seat, Samantha's aunt, Lynn Crocket, stepped to the podium to deliver the eulogy. She had to pause at times in order to steady herself or wipe a way a tear. She spoke gently, but her words conveyed strong emotions.

> The senseless act that took Sam away is so wrong and without the outcome that I so strongly believed in. We all have to choose which works for us to get through our loss. Personally, I choose laughter because when I hear Samantha's name, I am reminded of her contagious laugh. It could brighten any room, any mood, just when she started to giggle.
>
> From the moment Samantha was born, she had my brother's heart. They had that special bond only shared by father and daughter. I remember times when Sam would get in trouble. He would ground her and talk all tough about how he was going to discipline her. The next thing you know, she had a new computer, new clothes, new something.

Many of those listening laughed softly at the irony, thankful for the opportunity to have an outlet for their grief. Crocket, too, paused for a sorrowful laugh as she thought of Samantha's relationship with her father.

> She knew she had her daddy wrapped around her finger. Oftentimes he did without just so he could provide for her.
>
> The last time I saw Samantha is a memory I am blessed with. Back in January, one night she came over with Duane to borrow sleds.

Samantha introduced Duane and said she'd just been hired at a coffee stand, a job she had been trying to get for quite some time. She was so happy and so excited about it.

The whole visit was only about 20 minutes or so. We said our "I love you's" and gave each other hugs.

Crocket paused to fight back tears as her voice faintly wavered.

"Had I known what the future held, I'd have never let her go," she barely managed to say as she choked up, struggling to finish. Her words had been prepared, yet they were still so painful to utter.

"Although what happened to Samantha is tragic and sad, it doesn't have to end sad," Crocket said somberly. "She didn't have a sad life. She was happy and she was loved. She will be forever in our hearts."

After Crocket's ardent comments, a local violinist played a touching tribute to Samantha while a ten-minute slide show of her life displayed on the screen behind him. When the violinist and slide show finished, Novakovich read part of a letter that James Koenig had written to his beloved daughter.

It saddens me that our time here on earth is over for now, but I know that you are here with me in spirit, and we will be together again one day. The lives that you have touched, without even meeting them, has been amazing, as only an angel like you could have done. I know that you are watching over me, and you need to know that I will be fine because you will always have my heart, as I have yours.

Then Robert Crocket, Samantha's "Uncle Bob," approached the podium. Faced with unspeakable despair, he hoped that humor might penetrate the atmosphere of sadness that weighed so heavily on the hearts of all in attendance.

"If you knew Sam," he said with a forced smile, "she was always cracking jokes. And if you didn't know Sam, she would make you feel like you were an old friend – and then she'd crack jokes. Sam could talk and giggle at the same time, and it would run together."

Now Crocket shifted to a more serious, yet still positive, tone, addressing James by his affectionate nickname, "Son," short for Sonny.

> She's in my heart and I'm better for it. She's in yours too, and if there's any good to come from this, let Sam make you a better person by laughing more, smiling more, and sharing happiness with others. Sam would want you to be happy.
>
> Sam was her dad's girl. He would do anything for her. In the past three months, Son has had a parent's worst nightmare. He faced each day and each challenge with the goal of finding Sam. And against the odds, he refused to give up or accept defeat.

Addressing his next words to James, he choked up as he continued.

"Thank you for being a great dad. No one I know could be as strong. It's a show of your true character. Sam is proud of you."

Then he gestured toward the packed auditorium, acknowledging the outpouring of support from the local community.

"With the help of all of you," he said, "Sonny found ways to push forward, generate positive results, and deal with information no one should have to deal with. Everyone left their comfort zone to help. They gave time and money and prayers and hopes. All in an effort to find Sam. Alaskans are unique. They help. They give until it hurts. Whatever it takes. Your support is what defines us as proud, strong Alaskans. Thank you all for being there."

Crocket concluded his remarks on a hopeful note, doing his best to bring out the positive from an event so hurtful and tragic.

"We have to decide how to react to the events that led to today. Sam would want us to keep doing amazing things. How we react is our decision. Instead of blaming or complaining, Sam would want us to seize the day, live life to the fullest, make someone's day brighter, laugh, and smile more."

Then he turned to James one last time.

"Son, Sam was your girl, and now, she's all of ours," he said, holding back tears. "She's all of Alaska's girl."

After the bittersweet ceremony concluded, the celebrants stepped outside into the parking lot, joining James Koenig, clad in a leather vest with embroidered lime-green angel wings on the back, as he released dozens of green balloons in honor of Samantha. The crowd clapped and cheered, letting loose its collective grief as the balloons floated toward Heaven, growing smaller and smaller as they disappeared into the clear, blue sky.

(Anchorage, 2011)

In April or May 2011, Keyes rides his bike to Point Woronzof Park in West Anchorage after the park has closed. Around 10:00 p.m., he targets a young couple in a parked car, planning to "snipe" them from the woods using a rifle equipped with a home-made silencer. But his plans are disrupted by an APD patrol cruiser that stops to tell the couple that they need to leave the park. Keyes is still willing to proceed with the shooting and resolves to shoot the policeman before shooting the young couple, but then an APD backup unit shows up too.

Recounting this near-killing a year later, Keyes is nonchalant about the details.

"It could have got ugly, but fortunately for the cop guy, his backup showed up. APD is really good – all by the book and stuff – and that's about the time I got a police scanner because I almost got myself in a lot of trouble on that one . . . almost pulled the trigger with him there. Anyway, as soon as his backup showed up, I decided I better call it a night and got back on my bike and took off."

He tries again in May, after burying a shovel and Drano as a kill-kit in a garbage bag in the woods near a nature trail leading to the North Fork of Eagle River. He picks the area due to its popularity with kayakers and rafters. He stakes out the parking lot for the trail's fee station and restroom and plans to kill whoever happens to show up.

"I was out looking for trouble. The plan there was, I had that parking lot staked out, waiting for somebody after it got fairly late. I was going to take them and use the cutoff tool, lock the gate with a padlock, and do my thing [kill them] there in the parking lot, and I had the Drano and shovel stocked up there as a way to get rid of the body if I needed it. I don't know why. I guess I was just itching for trouble. I knew I was going back East."

On June 2, Keyes catches a flight from Ted Stevens Anchorage International Airport to Chicago, legally declaring and securing his Ruger 10/22 Charger handgun in his checked baggage. A few days before, he had sent Sarah to stay with Tammie for two weeks. He told her that he would be spending some time at his New York property, planting and clearing trees and generally fixing it up. Tammie had been surprised, but she was happy to see Sarah and did not question the reason for his trip east.

Like a tourist looking forward to a long-awaited vacation, Keyes tingles with excitement about his new trip. But he is not looking forward to rest and relaxation. He is traveling to feed his addiction. He needs to feel the rush of the hunt, the thrill of the kill.

As with prior flights he has taken to other destinations, traveling never fails to strengthen his disbelief in God. Innocent people, even little kids and infants, died tragic and sometimes violent deaths every day. Yet, he repeatedly flew safely across the country to kill complete strangers in cold blood. The fact that he can commit such acts with impunity reaffirms his atheist beliefs. After all, if God really exists, how could He possibly allow these things to happen? How can such evil deeds go unpunished?

Once again, he arrives safe and sound at his destination. After claiming his bags in Chicago, Keyes rents a car from Hertz and drives to Indiana to visit family for a few days. From Indiana, he drives to his property in Constable, New York, before heading on to Vermont. On June 7, he checks into Room 216 of the Handy Suites hotel in Essex that he stayed at during his last trip to Essex in 2009. He is now nearly 1,000 miles away from Chicago. He pays for the hotel room using a credit card issued to Keyes Construction.

He obtains a three-day fishing license and fishes on Lake Champlain by Burlington. Though he does not realize it at the time, he later learns that Burlington, Vermont, was the birthplace of one of his idols, Ted Bundy. After fishing, it is time to reclaim one of his kill-kits. He returns to the Woodside Natural Area near the Woodside Juvenile Rehabilitation Facility, walks to the farthest point of the trail's loop, and digs up the orange, five-gallon bucket that he buried there two years earlier.

Twenty

On April 30, 2012, Keyes met with Kevin Feldis and Special Agents Jay Sherman and Thom King from the Bureau of Alcohol, Tobacco, and Firearms. Although happy to hear that, following his psychological evaluation, he had been found competent to stand trial, Keyes reiterated his desire to speed up the judicial process so that he could quickly receive the death penalty.

"If you're willing to work with me to make things happen that I want to see happen, then I can make your job easier for you," he promised.

His curiosity about the status of the recovery of the Curriers' bodies soon got the better of him.

"So what is the deal with the Curriers as far as the investigation? Where are they at, the people back east?"

"They're still digging," Feldis replied, "but they haven't found the bodies yet."

Keyes's eyes widened in surprise.

"You're kidding! Are you sure they have the right house?"

Feldis hesitated as he considered how best to answer.

"I think the concern, Israel, is that they may not be in the house anymore," he explained. "The house was demolished and stuff was carted away."

Keyes sat speechless, clearly stunned by the news.

"Wow," he murmured after a few moments. "That is crazy. I'm amazed that if they loaded the bodies onto a dump truck, nobody noticed that."

As the interview continued, Keyes spoke proudly about a home-made silencer that he had built in his shed out of parts obtained from Home Depot.

"I had big plans for that gun," he laughed.

Feldis tried to get more specifics about his "big plans."

"I don't know if I should go into my big plans," Keyes replied, "but suffice it to say I wanted a gun that I could carry under my jacket and put a silencer on pretty quick. It was my baby." He grinned and added a clarification. "*One* of my babies."

He described a target range that he had set up in the woods in the Chugach mountain range, in preparation to shoot out the tires of moving cars – one of his ideas for kidnapping future victims – by prac-ticing shooting at moving targets on a pulley from fifty yards away.

> One of the ideas I had for car-jackings [was to] shoot out their tires while they were pulling up to a stop sign or something, but I didn't find any good roads or places to do it. I kind of had it in the back of my mind, but when you get out in the backwoods people are kind of naïve and don't really expect anything like that to happen to them. So you don't really have to do anything as crazy as shooting out their tires, but that's one of the ideas I've had.
>
> Partly because you're on a road with the right amount of traffic, you can set up in the right spot, and sit there with binoculars and kind of stake out who is in the car. It's like shopping . . . if it's in the evening and there's not a lot of people around, it's on a backwoods road that gets a car every five or ten minutes, you shoot out someone's tires, she's by herself, and she doesn't have much choice but to stop. If you shoot it out with the .22 in the sidewall, she's going to have to stop in half a mile of where you shoot it out.

Apparently in a talkative mood, Keyes decided to disclose another multiple murder that he had nearly committed in Alaska: the ambush of the young couple in a car in the parking lot of Point Woronzof Park.

"That was a spur of the moment type of thing because Kimberly was out of town and Sarah was staying with her aunt for a couple of days," he recalled. "I was just out looking for trouble."

But he almost found more trouble than he wanted.

"The cops showing up brought me enough back to reality so I decided to wait until I went back east. Ever since I was a kid, white supremacist roots or something, I wanted to ambush a cop. But the way Alaska is set up is too risky. I just decided to go back to my old stomping grounds back east."

The unexpected appearance of the patrol cars was what prompted him to purchase a police scanner so that he would not be similarly surprised in the future.

Keyes stressed that using a gun to kill his victims would have been unusual for him. The only reason he planned on shooting the couple in the car was to see how well the silencer worked. Insisting that Bill Currier had been the only person he ever actually shot to death, Keyes explained that his shooting had happened because "I lost my cool for a few minutes," since Currier "was not cooperating," and "I was kind of stressed out a bit."

Currier's resistance "pissed me off because there was a specific way I wanted things done, a very specific way I wanted things to happen. And I had the whole thing planned out, and so when someone messes up that plan . . ." he trailed off before continuing. "It kind of even surprised me how I lost control that way."

The incident with Bill Currier seemed to perplex him.

No matter what I said or did it seemed like he wasn't taking it seriously anymore. Some people you can't really tell how they're going to react until they get pushed to a certain point and then there's a different person who comes out. And that's kind of what happened with him. Up until that point he'd been trying to talk me out of it. He was really belligerent and it pissed me off and I got the gun.

I went down to check on him and he had somehow started to get free and that's when we started to fight. He started trying to shove me around and stuff and I was just kind of laughing at him. But I couldn't get him overpowered enough to tie him back up. So that pissed me off because that's what the plan I had for him was to have him tied up downstairs.

After struggling with Currier, he went upstairs to get his gun. He returned about thirty seconds later.

"It was pitch dark in the basement, but I had a head lamp on. When I came back downstairs with the gun, it seemed like he was trying to find something to fight me with."

He shot Bill Currier several times as Currier stumbled blindly in the darkness. Keyes yawned while recounting the details of the shooting. Then he thought about the fact that the Curriers' bodies had disappeared.

"That's really weird that they haven't found anything yet. Maybe I didn't do it," he exclaimed with a laugh. "I jumped the gun on that one!"

Keyes thought about it a little while longer, then turned to Feldis.

"I want to see pictures," he said.

"Pictures of what?" Feldis asked.

"The crime scene."

"Explain that," Fedlis responded, "so I know what you're talking about."

"I want to see pictures. Of what they find."

"Of the bodies?" Fedlis asked incredulously.

"Yeah," Keyes answered nonchalantly, oblivious to Feldis's outrage.

On the other side of the continent, George Murtie called Jennie Emmons at the FBI, requesting Keyes's fingerprint and DNA records. In the face of obvious reluctance, Murtie pointed out that his investigative team had been providing extensive information to the FBI about the Currier case. He let Emmons know that he would have to contact the Anchorage Police Department if the FBI continued to be uncooperative with what he considered to be patently reasonable requests.

On May 2, Murtie received a call from Jeff Bell at the APD. Bell introduced himself as a member of the Israel Keyes task force. He had heard that Murtie contacted the APD about Keyes and wanted to know the reason for the call. Murtie explained that since the Currier and Samantha Koenig cases had intersected, he simply wanted to offer any assistance he might be able to provide to his counterparts in Alaska. Bell politely reciprocated.

Shortly after ending his call with Bell, Murtie heard that the FBI and U.S. Attorney's Office had been informed about his call to the APD, and they were not happy that he was "going around behind their backs" on the case.

Early on the morning of May 7, 2012, Murtie left his office in Essex and drove to the Casella Waste landfill in Coventry, arriving just before the FBI's Evidence Response Team appeared shortly after 10:00 a.m. Nearly two dozen FBI agents arrived with ATVs and equipment trailers, joined by the Vermont State Police's mobile crime scene command post. Tasked with searching through tons of trash, the team of investigators spent much of the day erecting tents, setting up generators, and installing fencing along the perimeter of the area to be searched. Having traced the debris from the demolished farmhouse in Essex to the landfill in Coventry, investigators hoped to at least find partial remains of the Curriers somewhere in the mountain of garbage.

Murtie knew that it would be a difficult job searching the immense landfill, but it needed to be done, and as a Christian and police officer, he felt that he owed it to Bill and Lorraine's families to help with the digging. The search team would be focusing on the backside of the landfill near the top of the trash heap since that was the area where the farmhouse debris had most likely been dumped. Clad in Tyvek suits and steel-toed boots, the team members donned goggles and two or three pairs of gloves. They also wore respirators, a necessary precaution since the landfill contained medical – and human – waste, and because they needed protection from the methane gas that leaked from the rotting garbage at constant intervals. Two paramedics were stationed on site as an additional precaution.

On a pleasant, sunny day with what would have otherwise been comfortable temperatures in the 70s, the heavily garbed group began the daunting task of their search. An excavator scraped away the landfill's top layer of dirt, approximately four feet deep, exposing the trash that had recently been buried beneath it. However, before they could make much headway, increasing winds of 25-30 mph necessitated an early end to the day's search efforts.

Several hours later, Murtie met with Jennifer Reading, a reporter from news station WCAX, and her News Director, Anson Tebbets. The two media members informed Murtie that they were aware of Keyes's involvement in the Currier case, and that Reading had already prepared a story about it. Concerned about the timing of the report, Murtie spent much of the meeting explaining that running the story would jeopardize the investigation and possibly ongoing investigations in other jurisdictions as well. By the end of their meeting, Murtie felt reasonably confident that Reading and Tebbets would hold off on the story until the status of the investigation became less sensitive.

May 11 marked the end of the first week of the Coventry landfill search, by which time the recovery team had established a uniform procedure for conducting the search. After the excavator dug up the trash from the target area or "hot zone," the debris was deposited on a large flat area, approximately 50 yards long, 15 feet wide, and 1 foot deep, an area called "the pad," before being sorted into three piles. The recovery team members positioned themselves along each line of trash with potato rakes and shifted through the rubbish looking for signs of human remains. Any bones found were collected and stored for analysis to determine whether they were animal or human. After clearing each pad, the team members underwent a decontamination process that included chemical washes for their boots and replacement of their gloves. Working at a steady pace, the team typically cleared two pads in the morning and two pads in the afternoon.

Another Keyes interview – this one nearly two-and-a-half hours long – took place on May 16 at the FBI's Anchorage office. At the outset, federal prosecutor Frank Russo detailed a plan by which Keyes would provide information on his victims in exchange for his case being kept out of state jurisdictions and his name kept out of the media. In response, Keyes reiterated his ultimate goal.

"I have no delusions how this is going to turn out for me in the end. I already know what the bottom line is for me. So all this other stuff between now and what ultimately happens . . . I could take it or leave it, at this point."

He emphasized the continuing need to maintain control of the dissemination of information about his crimes so he could shelter his family from the fallout as much as possible.

"My concern isn't for my own reputation. It's for people that I know, like my family. They've been getting threats from the public. And it's hard for them because they're all still convinced that I'm innocent. Everybody I've known, to a certain extent, you could say they're my victims, too, because they're going to have to pay for this for a lot of years to come."

Keyes resisted providing any specific information about victims other than Samantha Koenig and the Curriers. He worried about the effect such additional information could have on his young daughter.

"Things I've already done are going to affect my kid as she's growing up, even when I'm not around anymore. I'm just debating whether or not – how much I want attached to my name."

Just before 2:00 p.m. on Wednesday, May 23, 2012, Keyes appeared before United States District Judge Timothy Burgess in federal courtroom 1 accompanied by his defense attorneys. The hearing had been scheduled at the request of Keyes's attorneys so the judge could consider setting a new date for his trial. The defense lawyers alleged that they needed two years to review the voluminous investigative materials that had been produced by prosecutors during discovery. Assistant District Attorney Frank Russo countered that the bulk of the materials – some 90% of it – concerned false leads in the case, which would be easy to sort through "when you cut the wheat from the chaff." Russo pushed for a March 2013 trial date, just ten months out, rather than the two years requested by Keyes's attorneys.

"The family is in court today," Russo informed the judge, "and Mr. Koenig has indicated to me that he certainly wants closure."

In addition to Samantha Koenig's family and friends, a crowd of reporters and law enforcement agents sat in the gallery observing the proceedings. Four courtroom deputies stood between Keyes and the railing separating the spectator area. While the attorneys bantered back and forth, Keyes occasionally glanced around the courtroom as if making mental notes of who was there.

Jaqueline Walsh, one of Keyes's three defense counsel, stood to explain to the judge why the defense team needed additional time to prepare for trial.

"Our position is that at this particular juncture we're not . . . "

Suddenly, Keyes broke free from his steel leg shackles and jumped over the railing into the first row of seats in the courtroom gallery area. Amidst screams from the crowd of "Get him!" and "Kill him!" deputies tackled Keyes to the floor with a loud thud. As five deputies held the still-struggling Keyes in the second row of seats, one of them used a taser to subdue him so that he could be handcuffed. As abruptly as it had started, within seven quick seconds the escape attempt was over.

Deputies later discovered that Keyes had pulled off the chain from one of his ankle-cuffs, but they could not explain how he had managed to do so.

"I've been doing this for 20 years and have never seen one pulled like this," said perplexed supervisory deputy David Long.

As a result of his escape attempt, additional restrictions were immediately and permanently placed on Keyes. He had to wear full restraints whenever he ventured outside of his cell, and two guards were required to accompany him at all times. In addition, the cell next to his would henceforth be kept "empty and secured at all times" to prevent Keyes from seeking the help of a neighboring inmate.

Two days later, three U.S. Marshals ushered Keyes into the same courtroom and chained his handcuffs and leg shackles to the floor. Wearing the red prison jumpsuit indicative of a dangerous inmate, he gazed into the gallery as Samantha's Koenig's parents and other family members filed into the room. Shortly afterward, Judge Burgess strode into the courtroom. Frowning down on everyone from his seat behind the judicial bench, he admonished Keyes that further escape attempts would result in him being fitted with additional shackles as well as a gag, and he warned that it could also result in his being confined to watching the proceedings from a jail cell. Keyes meekly responded that he understood. The judge next addressed the reaction that had emanated from the courtroom gallery, chastising the spectators who called for violence during Keyes's escape attempt.

"Although Mr. Keyes's behavior was inappropriate," Judge Burgess dourly explained, "some of the comments were equally inappropriate. It's important for everyone to understand that what happened cannot happen, and it will not be tolerated."

As the hearing resumed, Frank Russo announced that the prosecution could be ready for trial even sooner than the previously contemplated ten months. He added that Keyes wanted an early trial date as well.

"It's our understanding that Mr. Keyes wants this to move forward more quickly," Russo explained. "If he does request a speedy trial, we can certainly accommodate that."

"Objection, Your Honor!"

Richard Curtner, Keyes's public defender, rose from his seat, clearly agitated by Russo's characterization of what his client wanted.

"Judge, you can ask Mr. Keyes himself," Russo countered.

"I oppose that," Curtner retorted, "you addressing Mr. Keyes."

Judge Burgess considered the matter for a moment.

"Asking a defendant about his wishes is not unusual," Burgess announced. "Indeed, it's incumbent upon the presiding judge to do so."

The judge turned to Keyes and asked him what time frame he wanted in terms of a trial date.

"If ten months is realistic, that's fine with me," Keyes answered and then added, "If it's realistic to set it sooner than ten months, that's also fine with me."

But Keyes's calm demeanor hid the fact that time was weighing heavily on him, and it was building to a crisis point.

Twenty-One

On May 24, clad in clay-red prison garb, handcuffed, and shackled at the ankles, Keyes sat at the end of a plain wooden conference table and joked with Bell and Payne about his escape attempt, particularly the taser gun that courtroom deputies had used to subdue him.

"I needed a good workout apparently," he giggled. "I have muscles sore this morning that I didn't even know I had. It reminded me of those late night infomercials they use to sell those machines that shock your abs and stuff."

Sitting across from Keyes at the table, Special Agent Payne, who in his 16-year career with the FBI had become well-versed in negotiations and the political logistics of working with multiple law enforcement agencies, tried to impress on Keyes that his escape attempt might hinder their ability to work together.

"That stunt yesterday in the court room did not go over well with the prosecutors," he warned.

"Why, were they afraid I'd actually get away?" Keyes said with a sudden laugh. "That would be embarrassing for them I guess. Lawyers just don't like excitement, that's all it is," he chuckled.

As the interview continued, Keyes steered the discussion toward his continued concern about getting the criminal proceedings against him "wrapped up as quickly as possible" to minimize the impact of his arrest on his daughter. He did not want her to see him linked to kidnappings and murders, he did not want her to remember him as a serial murderer, and he did not want his name linked to other crimes aside from the Koenig case. He was worried that without an appropriate level of information control, the criminal proceedings against him would "turn into even more of a three-ring circus."

Keyes tried to reassure the investigators that his escape attempt should not be construed as an indication that he no longer wanted to work with them.

"Yeah, what happened yesterday, ooh I'm a bad guy, but let's be honest, nobody really thought I was a good guy before that, so it's not like me escaping suddenly makes me untrustworthy. I was kind of untrustworthy before that," he said cackling loudly in response to his own joke.

Payne and Bell laughed along with him but reiterated that Keyes's escape attempt would make it harder to get other law enforcement agencies to cooperate with keeping information about his crimes under wraps.

"I've gotta believe that your next court appearance is going to be standing room only," Payne joked.

"There's probably going to be a lot of vigilantes guarding the door on that one," Keyes laughed in reply.

The next day, Payne, Bell, Russo, and Feldis met with Keyes and his attorney, Rich Curtner, at the U.S. Marshal's Office in Anchorage. The meeting started off with some light-hearted banter as Keyes walked into the interview room wearing his high-security-risk red prison uniform.

"Wearing red, huh?" Bell asked. "New clothes?"

"Yeah," Keyes replied with a chuckle, "finally got them back from the dry cleaner."

Despite its jovial start, the meeting soon turned more serious. Keyes had requested the meeting after learning that the prosecutors had not set up a meeting with the Department of Justice's Capital Case Unit, the entity responsible for evaluating potential death penalty cases. He expressed his confusion and agitation as to why "nothing" was being done to move his case forward. Feldis tried to assure him that CCU would be able to move quickly once the U.S. Attorney submitted its memorandum on whether to seek the death penalty. However, an agreement with U.S. Attorney Karen Loeffler that Keyes had signed at his attorney's behest on March 30, an agreement in which the Department of Justice agreed not to seek the death penalty against him in exchange for his cooperation in the Koenig case, was holding up the process.

"I never wanted this in the first place," Keyes stated, clearly exasperated after glancing through the document. He explained that he had only agreed to reveal details about the Koenig case based on Feldis's express representation that the March 30 agreement would not be relevant to whether the government recommended the death penalty.

"I feel like I was lied to," he said angrily.

Needing to reestablish his credibility, Feldis stressed that while the March 30 letter of agreement dictated whether the death penalty proceedings proceeded, the stumbling block could be easily removed.

"It can be as slow or quick as everybody in this room wants to make it," Feldis explained.

"It's a real concern here," Russo added. "We don't know where we are in this letter, and if we don't know where we are with this letter, we can't complete the package to Capital Crimes and give them the whole picture."

"Well, I want to go on the record right now that I do not want this letter on the table," Keyes replied angrily. "I want this letter declared null and void, and honestly, if I had known it was going to turn into this big of an issue, I would not have put my signature on it. I did not want to put my signature on it in the first place. So that's it. Let's take it off the table. Let's do whatever needs to be done."

Now Curtner, Keyes's court-appointed attorney, spoke up.

"Let's you and I talk about it before we do anything else," he said, attempting to caution his client.

Feldis did not want to the let the opportunity for clarification pass by.

"We need to know from you," he told Keyes.

"Well, I'll talk to him about it and we'll get back to you," Curtner replied.

"No," Keyes interjected. "That's off the table."

"Israel, just so I'm clear," Feldis continued, "your position is that you want the U.S. Attorney for the District of Alaska to recommend the death penalty in the Koenig prosecution?"

"Yes," Keyes responded resolutely.

Just as Keyes confirmed his position on the matter, one of his other attorneys – listening in via conference call – raised an objection and suggested that Keyes meet with all of his attorneys in person to discuss the matter further without any prosecutors or investigators present. Keyes immediately rejected the suggestion.

"The only thing I care about as far as the guilty plea is determined is when it is released, when it's made public knowledge," Keyes asserted. "Everyone who's been involved from the very beginning knows that I'm guilty, and knows what my plea is going to be and there's been no secret about it. There doesn't need to be a secret meeting or a secret consultation," he said in obvious annoyance.

Clarifying that his only concern was that his guilty plea not be made public until absolutely necessary, Keyes confirmed his desire for a quick imposition of the death penalty.

"I've known from the beginning," he explained, "once I saw the evidence, that's been my intent the entire time, pleading guilty. And I want CCU to recommend the death penalty."

————————————

The interviews continued on May 29 with Keyes meeting for nearly two hours with Payne, Bell, and Russo at the FBI's Anchorage office. Keyes focused on trying to establish a framework for how his case would be handled in exchange for his cooperation in helping investigators close some unsolved cases.

I was thinking there might be a way to disclose all this information to you, and to the FBI. And to some way ensure that we could work out some sort of agreement that, you know, I give you all the answers on these cases and families get closure and you find as many of them as possible. And in return for that, you know, I don't plan on being around a whole lot longer, but a really big concern to me is that my kid's going to be around. I don't want her to type my name into the computer and have it pop up. I already know stuff's going to come up. I'm just trying to minimize that at this point.

Russo attempted to assuage Keyes's concern, reminding him how they had been successful in keeping his name out of the media spotlight with regard to his involvement in the murders of Bill and Lorraine Currier.

"We're taking a big step in Vermont," Russo told him, "saying all right, you know what, obviously it's Keyes who's solving the Curriers crime and we're going to give you what you need, but in return we're not going to say anything, we're going to keep things under the radar. We're not going to link it publicly and we're not going to make a splash in the media."

Keyes remained curious about the status of Vermont law enforcement's efforts to locate the Curriers' bodies. Payne advised that authorities were still searching for the bodies and that they might not be found anytime soon.

"Yeah, that's a lot of trouble to go to. I almost feel guilty," Keyes snorted with a remorseless laugh, "costing the taxpayers a lot of money to find them."

Bell tried to refocus the discussion on the goal of satisfying Keyes's concern about limiting publicity of his involvement in any murders he might confess to having committed.

"I think what I heard you say is that you're wanting to take responsibility," Bell said. "Your plan is take responsibility if you can figure out how to do this without getting the recognition."

"Right," Keyes replied. "My concern – the problem is nowadays the more stuff my name is attached to, the more likely it is that somebody's going to try to do some kind of stupid freaking TV special, or you know, you know how it is. Nowadays like with all this true crime bullshit that people are obsessed with . . . yeah, I am concerned about that, about someone connecting the dots on this."

Then he made a cryptic reference to his own death.

"If I'm dead, then the investigation from the federal government's point of view is pretty much closed," he said.

Disturbed by Keyes's remark, Payne stressed that the investigators still wanted to work with him and that in doing so they would be able to minimize media coverage of the case.

"The reality is that, if we're not able to do this with your assistance, I can't imagine being able to do this without generating a fair amount of publicity. I just don't think it's possible because it's going to be too large in scope and it's going to involve too many jurisdictions and too many agencies."

Russo followed up Payne's comments by appealing to Keyes's desire to spare his daughter from having to hear negative things about him.

"There may be some benefit at the end of this," Russo told him, where the media says that Israel Keyes killed 40 people based on some wild speculation, as opposed to he killed 10 and then also gave closure to those families as his sort of last effort. I mean, I know that doesn't matter to you – but it may matter to her."

As the interview continued, Russo pressed Keyes to share specifics about several murders he committed in Washington, murders that he mentioned in a letter that corrections officers had recently confiscated from his cell. Keyes quickly rebuked Russo's request.

"The problem I have with talking about anything related to Washington," Keyes explained, "is that I'm not playing ball with the right people because I'm almost positive those are not going to be federal cases."

He did not want to get into the facts about the Washington murders until the federal matter involving the Koenig and Currier murders had been ironed out.

"There's a big difference between state and federal, and it seems like Washington might be state, and if I give it all out now, particularly anything about Washington, that could seriously compromise my future options."

Then Keyes changed the subject, joking again about his escape attempt and the wrench it had thrown in the relationship he had developed with the federal prosecutors.

"That was not well thought out on my part. It wasn't a high probability of success in the best of circumstances. There was like half a football team of U.S. Marshals between me and the door," he bellowed with laughter.

Department of Corrections personnel confiscated two letters from Keyes's cell. He had written one of the letters to his brothers admitting that he was a serial killer, but letting them know that he was not sorry for what he had done. In the other letter, a rambling 10-page stream of consciousness document written in all capital letters with no punctuation or paragraph structure, he described six murders that he had committed, as well as the accompanying sexual assaults. The letter included reference to the Currier and Samantha Koenig murders.

Along with the letters, prison officials made a disturbing discovery. Keyes had been drawing pictures on his cell wall using his own blood. The pictures included eleven skulls, under one of which, Keyes wrote, "We are one."

On June 1, 2012, George Murtie and Deputy State Attorney Mary Morrissey conducted a telephone interview of Keyes aimed at confirming his involvement in the Currier murders. Their requests for a face-to-face interview had been rejected by the FBI, so this would be the closest they would be able to come to him. Morrissey asked him a series of questions designed to elicit specifics about what the Curriers were wearing, as well as what was in their house when they disappeared. Keyes's answers more than convinced her that he had, in fact, abducted and killed Bill and Lorraine Currier just as he claimed. He had extensive knowledge of details that had not been made public.

Back in Alaska, Payne, Bell, and Russo sat at a table with Keyes in a sterile interview room listening to Murtie and Morrissey's questions. Clad in an orange prison jumpsuit, Keyes fielded their questions through a speakerphone. After Morrissey finished her line of questioning, Murtie wanted to delve into the depths of Keyes's psyche to try to find out why he had become a serial killer in the first place.

"I'd really like to try to understand why you did this," Murtie began. "You didn't wake up one morning and decide that this is what you wanted to do with your life, did you? I've been in this business for 28 years, and I'm very interested in people and how they make the choices that they do."

The speakerphone was silent as Keyes thought for a moment before answering.

"The short answer is that I don't really consider myself all that different or all that special from hundreds of thousands of other people," Keyes replied. "All you have to do is type in a word search on any given porn site, and there's all kinds of people who have fantasies about rape and bondage and the kinds of things that I take to another level."

Murtie considered Keyes's answer, and then asked a follow-up question.

"As it was explained to me," Murtie said, "people who early in life – through neglect or abuse – feel that they don't have any control over their life develop control fantasies over the course of their life and some of them involve violence and inflicting pain. But the other side of the coin is, you're not a hundred thousand other people. You're you and you've got specific reasons for doing what you did."

Keyes sat quietly for a few seconds while he thought about how much to reveal to the faceless detective on the other end of the line.

"With me it's a combination of things," he began. "It's not just about the sexual fantasy, and it's definitely not just about the money, and it's not just about the adrenaline. It's all those things together, and that's what I get out of it. And once I did it, once I started, there was nothing else like it."

Though the pitch of his voice barely fluctuated, the pleasure he derived from the depraved acts he described was discernible though the speakerphone. Murtie jotted down some notes on his legal pad and then asked Keyes if he had heard of fellow Alaskan serial killer, Robert Hansen.

"Yeah, I know all about him," Keyes replied enthusiastically. "I probably know every single serial killer that's ever been written about. It's kind of a hobby of mine." This was the most animated Keyes had been throughout the interview.

After about an hour, Murtie thanked him for his time and the interview concluded. The call having ended, Keyes tilted his coffee cup up to finish the final drops. As he did so, his eyes lifted to the ceiling and fixated on something. He stared intently for about ten seconds, as if studying a possible means of escape, but he was soon led back to his cell.

Back in Vermont, Murtie and Morrissey had both been struck by Keyes's overall demeanor during the interview. Morrissey said,

"He answered everything very matter-of-factly. There was no real emotion or empathy whatsoever. He was just very cold."

"I would describe it as if I was talking to a contractor about the work I was going to have done, and he was describing the work he had done in the past," Murtie agreed. "There was no emotion or anything. It was just flat."

Murtie struggled to reconcile his department's need to interview Keyes in person with the FBI's refusal to allow direct contact with him.

Murtie made many requests to travel to Anchorage to interview Keyes, but the FBI rejected all of them. Since the EPD's entire case in the Currier investigation was based on Keyes's confession, Murtie and his men needed access to Keyes to properly build the case. However, that access was not being provided. Murtie also thought it unusual – almost strange – that the U.S. Attorney's Office would be directly involved in interrogating Keyes.

Even access to Keyes's discussions with other law enforcement was strictly limited, including hours of videotaped interviews between Keyes, Anchorage Police Department investigators, U.S. Attorneys based in Alaska, and FBI agents. It seemed as if the FBI had deliberately tried to keep the interviews hidden from Murtie and the other Vermont investigators. Indeed, Murtie did not even realize that the videos existed until he overheard two FBI agents discussing them while searching the Coventry landfill. When he was finally allowed to view the interviews, the FBI required that he do so at the local FBI office, and he was specifically instructed that he could not take any notes. The restrictions extended to the questions Murtie intended to ask Keyes during their telephone interview: all of Murtie's questions had been screened by the FBI ahead of time, and he was not allowed to record the interview.

What most bothered Murtie was the FBI's insistence that Keyes be prosecuted federally and not be tried for the Currier murders in Vermont. He believed that the Currier family deserved to be able to face Keyes in court and voice to him the impact that his crimes had on their lives. Since many members of Bill and Lorraine's family were in ill health, they would not be able to make the lengthy trip to Alaska to participate in the federal proceedings there.

The externally imposed restrictions and overall dynamics combined to create a frustrating situation that, at times, felt like an adversarial relationship, rather than a cooperative investigation among agencies working toward a common goal.

During the course of Iz's incarceration, Tammie and Sarah stayed in touch with him through letters and phone calls, typically talking to him once a week. The calls were usually spent discussing Sarah and day-to-day events in Neah Bay, but Tammie also teased him about trying to escape, something he was still embarrassed about.

"I don't know what I was thinking," he told her sheepishly.

Although she still loved him, Tammie was the only one in her family who actually thought that Iz was guilty of the things that he had been accused of doing. The rest of the family could not imagine him being able to commit such acts. In their minds, he was simply too nice of a guy.

During one of their conversations, Iz suggested that Tammie change Sarah's last name to protect her from the negative fallout certain to result from his crimes. He warned her that things were going to get worse, and she needed to forgive him for what she would eventually learn about him. He worried that none of his family or friends would be able to forgive him once they heard about the extent of what he had done.

Tammie tried to get him to share specifics about his other crimes, rather than making her hear about them bit by bit on the evening news.

"How many times am I going to have to sit your daughter down and tell her that there's another one?" Tammie prodded.

But Iz never wanted to discuss them.

All the while, Tammie grew increasingly concerned about him. Her sister living in Anchorage had visited Iz in prison and relayed that he was being treated badly by the prison guards. He had told her that the guards "hated him" and degraded him whenever they could, including leaving him outside in the cold for hours at a time without a coat. More troubling than that, Tammie knew that Iz would not be able to stand spending his life in a prison cell.

She was worried about what he might do.

Twenty-Two

On June 5, Murtie made the long drive to Parishville, New York, to observe the search efforts to find Lorraine Currier's Ruger revolver in the Blake Falls Reservoir. Murtie was the first to arrive at the reservoir shortly after 8:00 a.m. About fifteen minutes later, the FBI's dive team showed up at the scene, and it did not take them long to locate the gun. Armed with information provided by Keyes, divers recovered the Ruger at 10:30 a.m., near the same spot that they had found the barrel and bolt of Keyes's other gun during a previous search.

In an interview two days later, Feldis tried to turn up the heat on Keyes, telling him that the law enforcement team had done everything that they had agreed to do, while he continued to stall about providing them more information about other crimes.

"We all agreed that we weren't going to be sitting here in a year doing this," Feldis reminded Keyes.

"Oh believe me, I'm very well aware of the passage of time,"

Keyes replied. "I have my own definite agenda on that issue, but as I've said, I don't have a lot of control over it."

Control was at the heart of Keyes's concerns. It had always been something he craved and it was the one thing that he intended to maintain, no matter the degree, and despite his imprisonment. Early in his incarceration, he determined that he would wield power by controlling the amount of information he chose to share, by parsing out details of his various crimes only when and where he wanted.

Feldis understood Keyes's need for control and attempted to play off of that craving to coax more information out of him, starting with the name of his New York victim.

"But I think you have more control than you think," Feldis pointed out. "Only you decide what you want to tell us. You, Israel Keyes, sitting here today, control what you tell us."

Keyes was not convinced.

"I've already given up control of that to a certain extent," he said, "but it's still within my power to decide how that information gets to you. It's not in my best interest today because there's absolutely nothing I gain from it. There's no objective that I'm moving towards by giving you more information."

As the conversation continued, Keyes made an obscure comment about the circumstances in which he would be willing to share more information about his crimes.

"I've been thinking that the best route for me to give you all of the information you need might be a last minute thing. So I'm not around for the aftermath," he chuckled. "They can't prosecute a dead man."

And he remained adamant that his name not be attached to the murders he had committed.

"I'm worried that eventually my name is going to be attached to it. If there's a way I can protect myself from that and still get you guys what you need, then I'm going to do it. I don't need to be punished for these other things that I haven't talked to you about yet because all of these other states, they're not going to prosecute a dead man."

He voiced a particular concern about the anniversary of the Curriers' murder occurring the next day, on June 8, and what the Vermont authorities might say about the case. He wondered whether they would be able to resist the temptation of naming him as the Curriers' murderer.

"I'm not giving any names today."

"They're not going to find a body from what you've told us," Feldis prodded, "so . . ."

"No, I'm not worried about that," Keyes replied smugly.

"So if you're not worried about it, it sounds like you have nothing to lose," Feldis urged. "I'm asking you for the most minimal thing that I think keeps us going in the right direction. We told you what we thought could help today."

"Yeah, I'm sure it'll help somebody," Keyes laughed, but he remained steadfast in his refusal to give any more information.

On the one year anniversary of the disappearance of Bill and Lorraine Currier, their family members gathered to remember them. The family recalled how Bill and Lorraine's ten nieces and nephews and eight great-nieces and -nephews "filled their home with laughter and love." They shared how Bill had been dubbed the "fun" uncle since he often shared video games with his nieces and nephews.

They lovingly recalled Lorraine's cooking skills, including her traditional French meat pies, which were always a hit during holidays. Bill's side of the family had grown so attached to her that they often joked that if Bill and Lorraine ever broke up, his family would take Lorraine.

Meanwhile, Vermont law enforcement continued to work the case, with the search effort at the Coventry landfill now in its sixth week.

"The case remains a top priority," Chittenden County State Attorney T.J. Donovan stressed. "This is a priority for the Currier family, the town of Essex, and the state of Vermont."

---

202 • DEVIL IN THE DARKNESS

As the digging continued in Vermont, Keyes met with Feldis and Russo in Anchorage. The two prosecutors hoped that this meeting would finally convince Keyes to detail his prior crimes, including and most importantly, the murders he committed prior to the Curriers and Samantha Koenig. Russo began the meeting by presenting a step-by-step plan about how Keyes could get what he wanted – prosecution only in Alaska and an expeditious imposition of the death penalty – in exchange for providing the information the investigative team wanted.

Russo pointed out that the U.S. Attorney in Alaska had a good relationship with the Vermont U.S. Attorney, a relationship key to getting Vermont's cooperation in not divulging Keyes's name in the Currier case. Russo also stressed that the FBI denied requests from Vermont investigators to interview Keyes so that the FBI could maintain control over any information he chose to share. He advised that they would like for him to divulge the names of his victims, if known, a brief description of the victims, and his best recollection of where he buried or otherwise disposed of their bodies.

"We have to assume that everywhere you've traveled, you've killed somebody," Russo said, explaining that if a local law enforcement jurisdiction at any of those locations could not provide assurances that one of their investigators "won't go off the reservation and try to make a career for themselves," then the FBI would simply decline to work with that jurisdiction on its pertinent missing persons case.

"I don't have any problem with the plan," Keyes replied pensively, "but I don't see any reason why I should participate in it until I see what happens with the information I've already given you."

He looked around the room studying the faces of Feldis and Russo as he continued.

The concerns I have with the plan is that you're adding more fuel to the fire by talking to other jurisdictions, especially if I'm giving you all of the other jurisdictions up front. My concern is that it's going to slow the process down. All it's going to take is one jurisdiction to balk at it and not go along with it.

I somewhat regret talking about Vermont in the first place. That

was, in my mind, the most critical piece of information that I had in
that it was fairly recent. And because of things that we all know have
happened since I did that – the demolition of the house and the
disappearance of the bodies – that's not something that I could ever
have predicted happening. But what concerns me at this point is how
involved that whole process in Vermont has become.

Keyes laughed as he mentioned the timing of having revealed the
facts of the Currier murders only after their bodies had most likely
been lost forever. After all, without a body, it would be extremely hard
to prosecute a murder case. The irony of the situation amused him.
Then he remembered something that Russo had mentioned during an
earlier interview.

My other concern is that you talk about closure to the families, and
closure comes when they find a body. Vermont was less than a year
ago, and I'm just concerned that in talking about other jurisdictions
and other locations that it's going to be a search on scale with what
they're having to do in Vermont, at least, if not more.

I realize that knowing is the first step, but the fact of the matter is
that they're going to want to find something. Vermont was different,
and frankly, things that happened in Vermont were very different from
things that I'd done prior to that. So there's not going to be as many
details that anybody knows besides me. There's just not.

The reality is if I hadn't said anything about Vermont, even with
my computer, you'd probably never have put two and two together.

I understand that closure is important from your point of view, but
I don't think on those terms from my point of view. I have no
delusions about how this will turn out from my end. I already know
the bottom line for me, so all this other stuff between now and then, I
could take it or leave it at this point.

He admitted that part of him would actually enjoy talking about his
other victims, but he would not do so until he knew what the time
frame would be for imposing the death penalty.

"From my perspective, it's damned if do, damned if I don't," he said. Much of his vexation arose from the fact that most of the other murders would not fall under federal jurisdiction, and he did not want multiple prosecutions in multiple state jurisdictions.

"That's still my concern. I might end up with a nightmare situation with things dragging on for who knows how long."

Feldis assured him that under the Travel Act, if he left Alaska and committed a crime in another state it would still be under federal jurisdiction if he had actually planned the crime in Alaska.

"Let's meet halfway," Feldis suggested, "give me something I can take to the bosses to satisfy them."

"There's other stuff in New York which in a way is related to Vermont," Keyes offered. But something else worried him as well.

I'm not a stupid person. I'm not grandstanding. I'm not in this for the media attention. I don't want anything happening to my family, you know, misguided vigilantes who think that they're actually helping or whatever.

Everybody I've known, to a certain extent, you could say they're my victims too because they're going to have to pay for this for a lot of years to come. For my perspective, it'll all be over pretty quickly. Because in the big picture it's not really going to be that much time if things move forward like we'd all like to see it.

Silence enveloped the room, settling in as if everyone was waiting for someone else to speak. After a few minutes, Keyes broke the silence.

"Tell you what," he said slowly, stopping often to pause in thought. "For now . . . I can . .. first of all, do I get a cigar today?" he laughed.

"If it'll help," Russo said echoing his laughter.

"If I get a cigar . . . what I can do is I can give you something . . . I'm not going to give you a body yet, and I'm not going to give you anything that happened on that trip."

Russo rushed out of the room, returning minutes later with a cigar. He handed it to Keyes and lit it.

"So New York," Keyes said exhaling deeply, "I don't remember the exact year, but there was a bank robbery in Tupper Lake, and that was me. I know why I was there, but anything other than the bank robbery I don't want to talk about right away."

Feldis frowned in annoyance.

"I thought you were going to tell us about New York," he said, "that there's a body in New York."

"Well, as I say, there are more things I could talk about in New York, but I'm not going to go into specifics right now," Keyes replied coyly.

He studied Feldis's eyes with curious amusement, exploring the extent of his exasperation. Several minutes passed by as the smoke from Keyes's cigar drifted lazily throughout the room, while the three men exchanged expectant glances in uneasy silence. Finally, the muffled sound of Keyes's voice came through as he held the cigar in his mouth.

"There's one in New York," he said.

Feldis perked up.

"Okay, so we can tell them that there's a body in New York?" he asked.

"Well, yeah, there's *remains* in New York," Keyes clarified.

"Someone from New York, or that's where the remains are?"

"That's where the remains are."

"But not a New Yorker?"

"I'm not going to go into that," Keyes grinned.

"Is it someone from Vermont?" Feldis pressed.

Keyes's grin grew larger.

"I'm not going to get into that," he repeated.

Now Russo tried.

"Male or female?" he asked.

"It was on the same trip as the robbery," Keyes began, elaborating on the circumstances.

There weren't a lot of people there. It started out I was going to just talk to one teller, but when I saw that there weren't a lot of people there, I just took over the place.

My initial intention in Vermont was just to check on the guns. I wanted to make sure they were still ok[ay]. I was going to dig them up and rebury them somewhere in Maine. I hadn't really planned on doing something in Vermont for sure. Originally, I was thinking that I'd go further east, like to Maine or something.

"The remains – are they buried?" Russo asked. "Will they be retrievable?"

"Good question," Keyes replied, his own curiosity piqued, "there should be something."

"I wish you'd give us more specifics about the New York murder," Feldis said.

"Well, I'm not going anywhere," Keyes said with a smile.

"Things I've already done are going to affect Sarah even when I'm not around anymore. For right now, it's still in my control. If we can keep the sensationalism to a minimum, then I don't have a problem closing some cases."

"Well, you know, if you helped bring closure," Russo pointed out, "that would be something positive that Sarah could remember about you."

Keyes weighed Russo's words in his mind.

"I'll think about it and figure out what I want to do," he said. "As of right now, I'm still not guilty of anything," he laughed. "That's something I have to decide. Do I want to be guilty or not guilty. I'm not giving any more information until I see what happens."

As the interview wound down, Russo pulled out a photograph, a still shot taken from a security camera at the Tupper Lake bank that Keyes had robbed. The photo showed a poorly disguised Keyes sporting an obviously fake beard. The three men shared a laugh about the amateurish disguise.

"I've got to say, they've definitely improved surveillance cameras," Keyes joked.

"Where'd you get the hair for that beard?" Russo asked. "Is that real hair? Where'd you buy real hair?"

"You don't have to buy real hair," Keyes replied. "Hair's free. Everything's free if you take it," he smirked.

Russo and Feldis exchanged startled glances.

"One way or the other, this will all be wrapped up soon," Keyes said with a wink as guards escorted him back to his cell.

Twenty-Three

On July 12, Frank Russo sent an email to Mary Morrissey to update her on federal investigators' attempts to identify Keyes's other victims. Russo expressed disappointment in not making headway in identifying the New York victim.

The discouraging thing is that the FBI basically has hit a dead end with the NY victim. All reported missing people for that week on the eastern seaboard have been checked out by FBI headquarters, and they have ruled them out. So, it appears that the person in NY was either never reported missing, taken out of NCIC, or mistakenly cleared. If this process has taught us anything it is that there has to be a more comprehensive system for accounting for missing adults in this country.

We do have a possible Texas victim, and a couple possible in Washington that we may show him. Hopefully we'll have some more insight on Tuesday and I'll let you know. Sounds like the dump is almost at a dead end? He asked about it on Friday and then said, "Boy, I really wish I could take that one back.

On July 18, George Murtie and an assembly of other law enforcement personnel met with the Currier family at the U.S. Attorney's Office in Burlington. During the meeting, the family learned for the first time about Israel Keyes and the Samantha Koenig case. Murtie and his colleagues were careful to emphasize that Lorraine had fought Keyes and that Bill had died trying to protect Lorraine, but they also stressed that the new information needed to be kept confidential to give similarly situated families the best chance of learning the fate of their loved ones. Murtie found the family members to be "strongly supportive of law enforcement" but "extremely suspicious" of the media covering the investigation.

Back in Alaska, based on his earlier discussions with Keyes, Frank Russo prepared a letter outlining a settlement offer from the U.S. Attorney's Office in connection with the Currier case. Under the terms of the settlement, Keyes would plead guilty in Alaska and be prosecuted there, rather than in Vermont state court. The letter spelled out the specifics of the proposed settlement:

> First, you agree to accept responsibility by pleading guilty to a federal charge of Carjacking causing death . . . In a separate sealed plea addendum, you would agree to cooperate with the United States by providing complete information concerning all of the uncharged murders and crimes you have committed. Initially, prior to entry of plea, you will provide the number of total murder victims and the jurisdictions (towns or counties) from which they were taken, as well as the jurisdictions (towns or counties) where the victims' bodies were disposed.
>
> The purpose of this information is twofold. First, it will be included in the confidential death penalty memorandum forwarded to the Capital Case Review Unit in the Currier case. Second, it will allow FBI headquarters to reach out to those jurisdictions to secure their agreement that you will not face federal, state, or local prosecutions for those crimes. . .Should any of the jurisdictions involved not agree to your request for non-prosecution in their

district, you would be relieved, under the agreement, from providing any further information about such victim.

In addition to these assurances, the United States would also agree to move the Currier case to sentencing as quickly as possible.

The next day, the FBI terminated its recovery operations at the Coventry landfill. Despite a tedious search that had spanned 51 days over an 11-week period, the recover team finished empty-handed. The remains of Bill and Lorraine Currier were never found.

On July 20, prosecutors and FBI agents held a press conference to reveal for the first time publicly that Bill and Lorraine Currier's mysterious disappearance had been the result of abduction and murder. George Murtie, Essex Police Chief Brad LaRose, local FBI office head Daniel Rachek, Chief Deputy State Attorney Mary Morrissey, and Lt. John Flanigan from the Vermont State Police filed into the briefing room in the Federal Building in downtown Burlington alongside Chittenden State Attorney T.J. Donovan and the U.S. Attorney for Vermont, Tristan Coffin. Over a dozen journalists awaited them. Donovan stepped to the podium first.

"The evidence now establishes that, on the night of June 8 to June 9, Bill and Lorraine Currier were abducted from their home and murdered by the person who abducted them," Donovan announced somberly. "The person believed to have committed the murders is in custody in another state and will remain in custody."

Hoping to assure the residents of Essex about the safety of their community, Donovan emphasized the utter randomness of the crime.

"Their murders were a random act of violence that occurred in our community. There is nothing the Curriers did in their personal lives that contributed to their deaths."

Following Donovan's remarks, U.S. Attorney Coffin read from a prepared statement, advising that "investigative leads from a federal investigation in another state" had led to the search of the Upper Main Street site in Essex Junction, which in turn led to the "massive effort" to search the Casella Coventry Landfill in Coventry involving 178 FBI agents wearing head-to-toe hazmat suits as they sifted through 10,000 tons of trash. With a total cost well into the seven figures, it had been one of the largest and most expensive searches in Vermont's history.

Coffin added that the suspect being held would remain in custody, but law enforcement would not be providing his name.

"More than that, I'm not going to comment on," Coffin said. Law enforcement would be strictly limiting the information released "to avoid compromising the investigation."

"Most important," Coffin read as he concluded his written remarks, "our hearts go out to the families of Bill and Lorraine Currier, as well as to their friends and to the community of which they were a part. This was an unspeakable tragedy, but hopefully these developments provide some level of closure for them."

Chief LaRose expressed similar sentiments.

"It's a bittersweet day," he said. "We have some information, but Bill and Lorraine are gone."

A reporter asked Coffin what motive the suspect had for killing the Curriers.

"He said that he felt compelled to kill by some uncontrollable force," Coffin replied, and then after reflecting further on the question, added, "Why someone acts like that, nobody really knows."

Donovan confirmed that the Curriers' mortal remains had not been recovered.

"Their remains were not found," he acknowledged regretfully, "but I will say this as well. We wish we could have found them for the family and this community above all."

Following the officials' comments, Donovan read a written statement from the Currier family, announcing in part, "We haven't yet made any plans for a public memorial service, but ask that you respond to this random act of violence with daily random acts of kindness in their names."

By the time the press conference concluded, South Burlington news station WCAX-TV ran a story reporting that anonymous sources had identified Israel Keyes as the Curriers' killer. One source had provided Keyes's name a few months earlier, and another source confirmed the name the day that WCAX released it. Although no law enforcement personnel in Alaska or Vermont would go on record confirming the report, Alaska media outlets quickly parroted the story.

Incensed after learning that his name had been linked to the Currier case, Keyes clammed up, refusing to speak any further with FBI investigators or other law enforcement. He felt betrayed by his interviewers.

Back on Colbert Street, the Curriers' neighbors expressed some relief that a suspect was behind bars in connection with the Curriers' abduction and murder.

"All of the indications that we heard before pointed to something like this," said Robert Brenneman, who moved into the neighborhood in May. "It's probably good for the family and it's good for the neighborhood. It takes some of the anxiety and the ambiguity out of the air, and that's a good thing."

Yet, many in the community shared the feeling that when the Curriers were taken, something else was taken away as well: a small town's sense of security that now seemed to have been nothing more than an empty shell.

"If someone would abduct someone from Colbert Street in Essex Junction, you're not safe anywhere," neighbor Randi Tomczak remarked dolefully.

Six days later, on the morning of July 26, Keyes and his attorney met with Frank Russo, Jolene Goeden, and Jeff Bell. His skin noticeably more pale, an inevitable result of being locked indoors virtually every minute of the day, Keyes began the one-and-a-half-hour meeting by inquiring about the timing of the sentencing phase of his trial. After Russo explained that the penalty phase would consist of a public hearing similar to the initial guilt phase, Keyes reemphasized his concerns about limiting or controlling the information that would come out about his crimes, and he expressed irritation about the WCAX story that had named him as the Curriers' killer.

"There's certain aspects of the things that I've done that I would prefer never became public," he advised, "as far as different things that were done with the bodies and the sexual assault stuff."

Keyes also elaborated on his reasons for having divulged details about the Currier and Koenig cases. He had thought that by volunteering the information, there would be no reason for it to be made public, but he had since learned the naivety of that belief, and he was angry about how the Currier case had been handled. Despite his insistence that local Vermont law enforcement not be involved if he revealed the location of the Curriers' remains, the FBI had allowed them to participate in the efforts to find the bodies.

"I'm getting a little bit ticked off at what's happening with the information that I've already given you, and I see no reason at this point to keep giving you information because I don't know what's going to happen with that. Quite frankly, I'm annoyed with you."

As the tone of the meeting turned more contentious, Russo tried a different tack.

"You blame us for the situation," Russo fired back, "I'm blaming you."

"I do blame you." Keyes retorted. "I told you from the get go – before I told you where the freaking bodies were left – I told you that I didn't want the locals involved, and the first thing you do is make a big scene and do a freaking archeological dig right along the side of a main road."

He remained insistent on maintaining some control over the situation. Involving the lead investigator from the Essex Police Department had given up too much control, and it was in direct contradiction of his ground rule that local law enforcement not be involved.

"You said that you would control it," he barked indignantly. "You haven't controlled it at all."

Now Jolene Goeden chimed in to try to reassure him.

"We have the ability to control it better now," Goeden insisted. "When you told us about the Curriers, we had no idea what we were dealing with. We didn't know there were seven or eight more bodies."

"You still have an opportunity to control that information," Russo added.

Their words did little to placate Keyes, and as they discussed various scenarios under which he could be charged in Alaska for the murder of Samantha Koenig or be charged in Vermont for the murder of the Curriers, he became even more frustrated. Hoping to change the tenor of the conversation, Russo sought to shift the discussion toward the possibility of a global agreement whereby Keyes would provide information about all of his victims.

"Obviously our preference, and I think yours too, is to wrap all this up globally with all the other crimes," Russo noted.

"Well, that's only if I can get what I want out of it," Keyes growled. "And that's looking less likely all the time. I still haven't been able to get a straight answer on any of it. I don't even understand how they can charge me in Vermont because Feldis told me this was a federal crime. That's the whole idea of me giving you the guns and the silencers and that crap because I thought it was all going to be federal, and now you're saying they want to charge me locally."

Russo was well aware of what Keyes wanted.

"My goal is not to get charged seven, eight different times or whatever, for the same thing," Keyes continued. "Apparently it's already out of my control. I'm already going to get charged twice."

Despite Russo's attempts to persuade him that he still had control over how the charges unfolded, Keyes remained unconvinced. The open nature of the sentencing hearing – the public airing of the details of his crimes – continued to bother him.

"If me looking for the death penalty is going to make this into a bigger circus than it already is, and they're going to take all of this information about all of the things that I've done and put it in a public hearing, then it's a problem," he said petulantly.

"Well, I can tell you the United States government controls what events and information is introduced in court," Russo said. "And I represent them. So I have absolute control over what evidence I put in."

"Right," Keyes replied with stoic sarcasm. "Well, that's good to know."

He frowned as he thought about the potential evidence being introduced at trial.

"I'm going to end up in fricking max lockdown year after year with you guys bouncing me around and around."

"Doesn't have to be that way," Russo assured him.

"Call it a premonition," Keyes countered cynically.

"Doesn't have to be that way," Russo repeated. "And we're trying to avoid that. Everybody in this room is trying to avoid it being a circus. You know, if we wanted to go ahead and just try to make you a villain, we could just go ahead and do that."

"I'm already a villain!" Keyes exclaimed in exasperation.

Russo's assurances had not quelled his concerns, not the least of which centered on how information about his other crimes would impact his family.

"Look, from an entertainment perspective, from my perspective, yeah, it would be really fun to have this stuff come out," Keyes admitted. "But, you know, I'm not trying to single-handedly give my mom a heart attack," he explained with a smirk.

"Everybody just makes too big of a deal out of this stuff. There's bigger problems in the world we could be worrying about right now," he said with an underlying tone of animus that reflected his growing disillusion about working with the FBI and federal prosecutors. It was beginning to dawn on him that he would not be getting the quick, simple death sentence that he wanted.

"Another factor that just occurred to me recently with the

sentencing portion is if whoever happens to be sentencing me knows that the death penalty is what I want, then there's a chance that there could be some reverse psychology going into play there and they're going to want to give me the opposite of what I want."

"Yeah, it's possible," Russo acknowledged, trying to avoid agitating him any further. "It's possible."

"There's just a lot of unknowns," Keyes said with a dispirited shrug.

Bell pressed him further, trying to talk him into revealing more information about his unknown victims.

"I can't see that there's anything for me to gain at this point," Keyes said, maintaining his reluctance to provide additional information. "It seems like whatever's going to happen is going to happen regardless. I don't know. I'm starting to think I'm more efficient than the government," Keyes said dejectedly.

"Well, I think you're good at planning stuff," Russo quipped.

"You're a planner and an organizer, we could use those skills now," Bell added with a good-natured grin.

"You know there's only certain things I like to plan," Keyes replied, cracking a half-smile. But the possibility of details of the Koenig murder being released still bothered him.

"What's going on with the Koenig case?" he asked. "I'm concerned that what's going to happen as soon as it gets to the point where I plea to that, then all of the media is going to want – it's going to be the same thing. They're all going to be clamoring for details, like what happened, and all of that."

"Capital Crimes has the memo," Russo advised. "It went in last week, but the U.S. Attorney wants something in writing nullifying the March 30 agreement not to seek the death penalty."

Keyes's brow furrowed deeply as he weighed Russo's words.

"So it sounds like you haven't recommended the death penalty," he remarked, the disappointment and disapproval readily discernible in his voice.

"I can't tell you what the U.S. Attorney recommended," Russo replied. "I'm prohibited from doing that."

Keyes frowned at what seemed to be purposeful foot-dragging in the death penalty proceeding.

"If I give you details on other crimes in other states, what's ultimately going to happen?" Keyes asked. "Is there some way we can work it out to where if I give you this information it stays sealed?"

Russo reiterated the need for a global agreement in which the information provided by Keyes concerning the Currier murders, the Koenig murder, and any other crimes, could be controlled and protected as much as possible from public release. But it was the Koenig case that most concerned Keyes.

"I don't care about what comes out about the Currier case," Keyes declared. "My point is I can try and limit the information that comes out on all this other stuff, but if the details of the Koenig case come out, then it doesn't matter how many other details we suppress on the other crimes."

In Keyes's mind, what he did to Samantha Koenig would be most damning to him in the court of public opinion and, more importantly, most damaging in the eyes of his daughter and other family members.

"If certain details of the Koenig case come out, then anything else doesn't matter," he reiterated. "That's kind of the worst case scenario, then everything else that I did before that is automatically going to be assumed to be just as bad."

As the interview wound down, Keyes made a troubling comment.

"Look, the bottom line is this: we already all know how this ends, so, you know, all I care about is what happens between now and whenever it ends. And if things don't go the way I want," he said, glancing around the room, "then I don't need you guys."

Bell, Goeden, and Russo exchanged startled looks. Without Keyes's cooperation, they knew they would have virtually no chance of locating and identifying his unknown victims.

"I've got to figure out what to do about this," Keyes added, the frustration never so clear as now in his voice. "This isn't working," he sighed.

Russo sensed that they were in danger of wasting all of the

progress that had been made during the untold hours of interviews they had spent building a rapport with him.

"In terms of what?" Russo asked earnestly. "Something we're doing? I mean, I'm trying to figure out to make sure…"

"Well, just everything," Keyes said, cutting him off impatiently.

As the interview ended, Russo had the overwhelming feeling that they were losing him.

Twenty-Four

At 2:00 p.m. on the afternoon of August 25, a memorial service was held at the Essex Alliance Church on Old Stage Road in Essex. Large framed pictures of Bill and Lorraine Currier lined the entrance of the church along with carefully arranged photo albums of their lives. Bill Currier's mother, Marilyn Chates, addressed the over 300 people in attendance.

"We have all learned that evil can visit even a small community like this," she said sadly.

The service concluded with a video of one of Bill's favorite songs, "Like a Bridge Over Troubled Water," by Simon and Garfunkel.

In lieu of flowers, the family members encouraged donations to assist in purchasing a bench in Bill and Lorraine's memory that would be placed outside the Brownell Library on Lincoln Street in Essex Junction.

On September 11, Alaska Department of Corrections officials found Keyes guilty of "possessing an object which had been modified to act as a handcuff key," an object confiscated in connection with a random search of his cell. He was sentenced to 60 days in punitive segregation, with 45 days suspended. His time in punitive segregation would begin on November 28.

———

On October 3, Keyes's counsel filed a Status Report with the court, claiming a need for additional time to prepare for trial, due in part to "the government's repeated contact with Mr. Keyes over the objection of undersigned counsel."

On the same day, on the other side of the country, members of the Currier family released a statement to their local newspaper, the *Burlington Free Press*.

> Although it has been a long road for our family, we continue to mourn in our own ways. We do feel lighter in our hearts, now that some closure has come to us, but the pain we have been dealt through this journey still lingers on.
>
> We are more conscious of our surroundings and people around us. We find ourselves looking at strangers and wondering what kind of person they are. We lay in bed at night and listen until sleep falls upon us.

———

In response to inquiry by a local Anchorage news channel, the Anchorage Police Department disclosed that the cost of investigating Samantha Koenig's disappearance exceeded $400,000 in overtime costs. By comparison, the cost of the average homicide investigation by the APD typically ran between $8,000 and $10,000. Police Chief Mark Mew explained that the Koenig case grew so expensive because "we thought it was a homicide that could occur if we didn't act quickly and work the case hard." In addition to the $413,186 spent on the Koenig case, the APD lost another $300,000 in ticket revenue during the investigation because of the hours the department's traffic unit officers devoted to the case.

Meanwhile, the October 15 deadline for the U.S Attorney's recommendation to the Capital Crimes Unit was fast approaching. As Frank Russo met with George Murtie and his colleagues in Vermont, Kevin Feldis was in Washington, D.C., filing a notice of intent to seek the death penalty with the CCU. Russo informed Murtie and members of the Currier family that the first official mention of Keyes's connection to Bill and Lorraine's murder would occur during the penalty phase of his trial for the murder of Samantha Koenig, a phase in which the Currier murders would be presented as an aggravating factor. Russo anticipated that Keyes would get the death penalty in the Koenig case, a sentence which would preclude him from facing trial in Vermont for the Currier killings.

Three days later, at Russo's suggestion, Diana Smith emailed James Koenig to let him know that he was not alone and that the Currier family was thinking of him and praying for him.

On October 23, Murtie received an email from Mary Morrissey that contained a forwarded message from Frank Russo in which he recounted a conversation that he had with Keyes earlier that morning. Keyes was trying to decide between two ways of moving forward: what he called "maximum publicity" or "minimum publicity." In the former, he would divulge all of the details of his crimes in pursuit of the death penalty, while attempting to "make a point" about how unnecessarily long the legal system takes to execute someone who not only deserves the death penalty, but who also actually wants to be executed. The minimum publicity route would be quicker as Keyes could take a deal with federal prosecutors by providing details of his other crimes in exchange for a sentence of life in prison. Under that scenario, Russo noted, it was obvious that Keyes intended to "get to a penitentiary where he could kill himself," as he had made numerous statements about not wanting to be in prison for any significant period of time. Russo's email also mentioned that Keyes's only regret was that "he wished he had killed more people while he was out."

On October 25, in a forested area north of Constable, New York, about five miles south of the Canadian border, Patrick Guagliano was enjoying his customary morning bike ride down a gravel stretch of Poplar Road when he noticed something strange.

"In the distance, it looked like a bunch of hunters in orange outfits walking around," he recalled. "There must be a lot of white-tailed deer up there," he had thought at the time.

As it turned out, the men wearing orange hats and vests were hunters of a sort, but they were not hunting deer. They were searching for evidence. Dozens of New York state police and FBI agents had converged on a run-down, red-and-green colored cabin and ten-acre property that investigators had recently learned belonged to Israel Keyes. Visions of unmarked graves on the property concealing the remains of unknown victims flashed in their heads.

"If he did have a couple of bodies to hide, there's a lot of places it could be up here," Chana O'Leary, the owner of a neighboring property, pointed out. Guagliano agreed.

"We're out in the middle of no man's land," he noted. "You could put anything and everything out there, and nobody would ever know it."

Although O'Leary lived nearby the property, for reasons she could not explain, she had always kept her distance from it.

"I've always been reluctant to walk onto that property," she said. "I couldn't tell you why. I drive by there almost every day."

The old cabin, constructed in 1890, had seen better days.

"It's old. It's shambled," Gugliano said. "The roof's caved in.

Unkempt, you might say. From the looks of everything, it hasn't been kept up in years. It's really in bad shape."

Even though Keyes had owned the property since 1997, none of the neighbors recalled ever having seen him there. Some remembered an Amish family that had stayed on the property for a couple of months approximately four years earlier, but none of them knew who the Amish family was or where they went after leaving. One neighbor had stumbled on what appeared to be a shallow grave a few months before the massive search, and he pointed out its location to an FBI agent during the search, but nothing relevant to the investigation was found.

By nightfall, the search was over, and all of the law enforcement personnel were gone, leaving the neighbors to wonder what was going on.

"To know that somebody of that caliber and that inhumane would have owned property here, it's just so bizarre because it's so peaceful here," said Connie LaBelle, another nearby resident.

———

By now, despite Keyes's recent misgivings and mounting frustrations, Feldis, Russo, and Goeden felt that they had made great strides in developing a relationship with him. Indeed, they believed they had forged a deeper bond with him than he had developed with his own attorneys.

Twenty-Five

On November 20, George Murtie received word that the United States Attorney General's Office would approve death penalty proceedings against Keyes by the first week of December. Immediately after the Attorney General's approval, the U.S. Attorney for Alaska would file paperwork seeking the death penalty in the Samantha Koenig case and, as planned, use the Currier murders as an aggravating factor supporting the imposition of capital punishment.

A week later, on November 27, Murtie learned that, due to a heavy caseload, the Attorney General's Capital Crimes Unit would now most likely not sign off on the death penalty for Keyes until sometime shortly before Christmas. Murtie also learned that, the next day, November 28, Keyes would be guiding FBI investigators via Googlemap to a location near Tupper Lake, New York, where he dumped another of his murder victims, a woman he had abducted from New Jersey in 2009 coinciding with his initial stay at the Handy Suites in Essex, Vermont.

On November 28, Keyes began serving his time in punitive segregation as scheduled, a confinement requiring that his cell be checked every 30 to 45 minutes. Assigned to Bravo module, Keyes's small, spartan cell had a concrete floor with matching white concrete block walls. Everything in the room consisted of a similar shade of white or stainless steel. The 8-by-11-foot rectangular enclosure contained a metal sink and counter area with a mirror directly across from the entry door. A metal toilet was attached to the wall just to the left of the sink, while a bunk bed sat immediately to the left of the door. An LED light served as the room's sole source of illumination, and a plexiglass window in the door offered the only view outside the room.

While in segregation, Keyes would spend 23 hours a day locked in his less than 90-square-foot cell. For someone who loved the freedom of traveling and so hated being confined, the torments of segregation were much more real than any speculative tortures awaiting him in Hell.

The next day, holding a cup of coffee in his chained, handcuffed hands, Keyes talked about his New York property with Bell, Goeden, Russo and Feldis. He said that he had not lived at the property since about 1997, but that he did visit it from time to time when he was in the area. And he was adamant that there was nothing on the property relevant to any crimes. No unmarked graves, no hidden bodies.

As the discussion continued, Goeden pulled out some photographs of one of Keyes's kill-kits. Technicians had found a fingerprint on a plastic tray containing ammunition inside the kill-kit bucket.

"There's a perfect right thumb print for Israel Keyes," she advised.

"Yeah, right," he replied in disbelief.

"No, there is," she assured him. "More CSI stuff."

"Wow, I'm impressed," he said half-heartedly. "Well, I'm disappointed in myself mostly," he added with an embarrassed grin. "I was kind of in a hurry, I guess. I was too lazy to dig a hole for that one. I just piled rocks on top of it."

"Were you planning on going back?" Feldis asked.

"Yeah, this summer, I would have had – that would have been a good trip," Keyes replied, letting out a hollow laugh.

Then he quieted and became contemplative.

"I still can't get over the whole disappeared house thing in Vermont," he murmured in muted disappointment.

Feldis tried again to push forward with an agreement whereby Keyes would disclose his other crimes, but Keyes continued to doubt that a satisfactory arrangement could be made, and he warned that he was "losing interest in the legal process."

Initially I thought there were ways that I could manipulate the situation, this case, all the related cases, to my benefit and on my timeline by withholding information and giving information out. And obviously, over the last few months, I came to the realization that I can't do that.

The problem is I don't have any typical demands and there's not anything you can offer me at this point, and I realize that now. Because of things that have happened over the last couple months, I just feel like there's a lot of information that I've given out to date that, 20/20 hindsight, I wouldn't have given out because I feel like now, no matter what I do, it's going to become public anyway. Whereas if I hadn't have given it out, it wouldn't have because you wouldn't have the information to give out in the first place.

As always, Keyes's concern about the release of details of his crimes stemmed primarily from the desire to keep his family from learning about it, especially his daughter.

"My kid is living in Neah Bay now and gossip is the town pastime there. So that's my concern right now."

However, as a token of good faith, he revealed that, in committing several murders in Washington state, he had used a Tanto folding knife with a four-inch blade that he had purchased at Walmart, and that there might still be blood on the inside of the knife case. He also disclosed that the bodies that he had dumped in a Washington lake would no longer be intact because they had not been contained in anything that would slow decomposition when he disposed of them.

Feldis tried to clarify what other weapons Keyes had used during his crimes. He asked whether Keyes used a gun while committing the Washington murders.

"Were either of those victims shot?"

"No," Keyes replied.

"No? Strangled?"

"No, the only person I ever shot was Bill Currier."

"Everybody else was strangled?"

"Yeah . . . or, yeah."

"Or? I don't want to have the wrong impression. So, everybody else was strangled, or was there something else?" Feldis asked in follow-up.

"Well, in one of the Washington things, it wasn't strangling. I hit somebody in the head."

"Did you mean to kill them, or was there a struggle and you hit them and they died?"

"No, I wasn't – I wasn't trying to kill them. I was just taking them out of action."

Russo mentioned that they had read something about that killing in one of the letters that authorities had confiscated from Keyes's jail cell.

"I didn't realize they were allowed to just take stuff out of my cell that I wasn't mailing," Keyes remarked. "That was a pretty big mistake on my part."

Feldis kept the topic going.

"Well, we know from that – that there was a couple in Washington state. A male-female couple. We read that in the note. Is that the same couple you took to the boat and dumped in the lake?"

"Oh, they went in the hole," Russo commented, recalling the contents of the confiscated letter. "They were buried."

"Yeah, that was a while ago," Keyes confirmed.

"Okay," Feldis continued, "and you had told us one time that it wasn't long after you got out of the military that you killed somebody, and it was a sort of feeling that you needed to do something. That it was hard to resist."

"Yeah, Neah Bay's a boring town," Keyes joked, flashing an alligator smile.

Keyes acknowledged that he had killed four people in Washington: two that he had buried and a male-female couple whose bodies he submerged in the lake. He also mentioned kill-kits buried at different locations in different states, including one in Washington and the one he had already told them about in New York. However, he was not ready to reveal the full extent of the kill-kits yet.

"I'll have to think about which ones I'm willing to part with," he laughed. "It all still belongs to me until you know about it."

He explained that he had disposed of the bodies in Washington in Lake Crescent, and he had dumped the bodies at a spot that was over one hundred feet deep. He had stayed near the edge of the lake, but the V-shaped bottom rapidly dropped off, going down to a depth of sixty feet just thirty feet from the shore. He had dumped the bodies at a spot deeper than his 100-foot depth finder could register. He used four or five milk jugs to sink each of them and now he was curious whether the bodies were still intact in light of the extreme depth and coldness of the water.

"It always had me curious as to what it would look like. I would think as deep as that lake is, it's probably sitting there just exactly as it was when it first touched down," he told them.

Pressed to reveal the location of another one of his kill-kits, Keyes referred in general terms to one that he had buried somewhere in Washington between Neah Bay and Seattle. Musing on the contents of that cache, he made a vague remark that would never be explained.

"I'm concerned about the little stuff that might be in it," he muttered, before pausing as if adrift in deep thought.

"Well, well, well . . . things you never thought you'd be talking about," he said softly while staring down at the table, his mind momentarily elsewhere.

The interview ended with Keyes mentioning the possibility of another meeting the following week. As the investigators left the room, Keyes finished the last of his coffee. He noticed something on his left shoulder and lightly brushed it off onto the floor as the padlocks and chains securing his handcuffed hands jingled. He sat back in his chair at the end of the brown conference table and stared down, once again lost in the labyrinth of his private thoughts.

At 7:00 p.m. the next evening, guards in the Bravo Module of the Anchorage Correctional Complex escorted Keyes to the prison law library. He spent the next two hours there, just as he had the previous two nights, and then the guards returned him to his cell at 9:00. At 10:13 p.m., just before lights out, the on-shift guards watched him as he prepared for bed. Nothing looked out of the ordinary. It was just another night in an endless stream of routine.

PART III: A Methodical Killer For A Modern Age

"So every bondman in his own hand bears the power to cancel his own captivity"

Julius Caesar, Act I, sc. 3

Twenty-Six

E arly on Sunday morning, December 2, 2012, shortly after the main lights flicked on around 5:57 a.m., corrections officer Lamont Wilson started the morning count and security check in the Anchorage Correctional Complex's Bravo Module segregation unit. As he came to cell 3, Wilson looked inside and noticed a strange red-colored streak on the floor. Peering closer, Wilson's eyes widened as he recognized the red substance. It was blood.

Wilson anxiously called out to the cell's occupant, but there was no reply. Grabbing his walkie-talkie, he requested immediate assistance from the prison medical staff while continuing to call to the unresponsive figure in the cell.

Within minutes, prison medical personnel arrived. After entering the cell, they pulled back the blanket from the inmate's bed and found him lying face-down, covered in blood. The inmate's body was rigid, his face was blue, and his pale arms were folded under his chest. City paramedics arrived soon afterward, and double-checking the inmate's absent pulse confirmed the obvious. Israel Keyes was pronounced dead at 6:13 a.m.

Keyes's left wrist had been slit open along the vein, and a small razor blade was found under his body. The blade was attached to a pencil to give it better leverage. Apparently not wanting to risk failing to bleed to death, Keyes had added a safeguard to ensure success in his suicide attempt. Lying on his stomach in bed, the position he usually slept in, Keyes had noosed a bedsheet around his neck and, with his heel pulled up toward his buttocks, he tied the other end of the sheet to his left ankle. The sheet had been purposely positioned so that when he lost consciousness due to blood loss, the force of his elevated leg lowering back down onto the bed squeezed the noosed sheet tightly around his neck, strangling him.

To delay the discovery of his body, Keyes even had the foresight to collect the blood as it flowed out of his razor-sliced wrist. Two milk containers and two cups filled with blood lay on the bunk next to his body. He had remained focused on the grisly task even as he grew increasingly light-headed, carefully catching the vital crimson liquid as it spilled from his veins, even as he slipped to the cusp of unconsciousness. And he had done it all while discreetly concealed under his bed covers. He had schemed and devised his own death with the same methodical planning that he had used to kill his victims. Indeed, the dual-level suicide worked so successfully that the medical examiner could not determine whether strangulation or blood loss was the primary cause of Keyes's death.

After the announcement of Keyes's death, prison officials revealed that he had spent weeks on suicide watch, but was no longer deemed a suicide threat at the time of his death.

"He had intended to hurt himself," Superintendent Bryan Brandenburg said, explaining Keyes's time on suicide watch. "We discovered that and put him on suicide precautions."

While on suicide watch, Keyes had been given a special gown and a suicide blanket, a thick, specially woven blanket that could not be used for strangling or hanging himself. However, a few months before his death, prison psychiatric staff determined that he was no longer suicidal.

Brandenburg could not explain how Keyes had acquired the razor blade he used to kill himself. Inmates in the segregation area in which Keyes had been housed were kept in their cells 23 hours a day. They were given one plastic, disposable razor to use for shaving in the shower, but they were transported to and from the shower in handcuffs and shackles, and the inmates were always required to return their razor after showering. Earlier in his confinement, Keyes had been restricted to an electric razor to prevent him from having access to a razor blade, and he was only allowed to use ink pens, which had to be checked in and out each day, rather than being given pencils. His cell was also searched on a daily basis. However, a prison log dated December 1 revealed that "15 razors" were brought into the 15-unit segregation area at 5:03 a.m. on the date of Keyes's death.

After lights out on December 1, a corrections officer had checked on Keyes every 30 to 45 minutes, and he appeared to be asleep under his blanket throughout the night. He typically slept covered by a blanket, so the on-duty corrections officer never felt the need to check on him beyond glancing into the cell as he passed by.

"What he saw when he looked in Mr. Keyes's room was the same thing he had seen on other nights on this shift," Bradenburg explained. "He was very devious, cunning, and manipulative" in the way he planned and carried out his suicide, Brandenburg said.

Wrapped within the blanket on Keyes's bed, prison officials found the crumpled, yellow pages of a legal-pad notebook covered with his handwriting and saturated with his own blood. The pages were immediately turned over to the FBI for analysis.

About five hours after the discovery of Keyes's body, Alaska authorities notified their Vermont counterparts about his death. Bill Currier's mother, Marilyn Chates, experienced mixed emotions upon learning that her son's killer had committed suicide. She initially felt that Keyes had "gotten away with it" by killing himself, but George Murtie's suggestion that Keyes was "facing justice in a different jurisdiction now" had been meaningful to her.

"So many thoughts have swirled through my mind," Chates said, "but at this moment I'm feeling that this probably is the best thing that could have happened. He will kill no more, and we will be saved from months, if not years, of trials and appeals."

Her thoughts also turned to Samantha Koenig's family.

"I hope will all my heart that the family and friends of Samantha Koenig feel the same, and pray that peace will come eventually to all of us."

When Diana Smith heard the news about Keyes's suicide, her first reaction was concern for the families still trying to find out where their loved ones were buried.

"Did he give any information about other victims before he died?" she asked hopefully.

While shocking in its finality, the news of Iz's suicide did not really surprise Tammie Hawkins. She had feared that he would kill himself rather than remain trapped in a cell. She had even mentioned it in a letter to Iz in July, writing: *If you are thinking about killing yourself, please don't. You can still help raise Sarah from prison.* Yet, during her final telephone conversation with him, he seemed to have been in a good mood. He was happy and upbeat, like his old self when they first met, and they had a wholly positive, light-hearted discussion. That had been on a Thursday or Friday. Then he killed himself on Saturday.

On December 2, federal prosecutors, police, and FBI agents held a press conference at the U.S. Attorney's Office in Anchorage to provide details about their investigation that they had been unwilling to share previously. Anchorage Police Chief Mark Mew explained why they had been so adamant about not disclosing more than bare bones facts during the investigation: it had been a condition demanded by Keyes in exchange for his cooperation.

"He was very, very sensitive to his reputation, as odd as that sounds," Mew explained. "And we had to keep things extremely quiet in order to keep him talking to us."

Mary Rook, head of the FBI's Anchorage office, confirmed that, in addition to Koenig in Alaska and the Curriers in Vermont, Keyes had confessed to killing four people in Washington and one person in New York. However, the FBI believed that, during Keyes's decade-long killing career, his victims numbered more than those eight.

"We believe there are other victims in other states. We are continuing our efforts to identify those victims," Rook said. "We have been analyzing financial records, travel records, any other records that are available to us over the last several years, to try and identify the course of his travels."

The investigators called Keyes "highly organized, highly methodical," and explained that his victims did not appear to have any characteristics in common.

"There really isn't any one type of victim," Jolene Goeden pointed out. "It's more about the circumstances and the situation rather than the specific victim. What we do know about him is that he worked alone. He traveled a lot. He was a loner. He would go to a state and get a vehicle and he would drive."

That was how Keyes had eluded identification for so long. And the longer he did so, the bolder he had become.

"He didn't commit his crimes in the same place over and over," Goeden noted, distinguishing him from other serial killers. "He didn't operate in his own backyard. He was very good at removing himself from a location where a crime was committed, traveling to a location, committing a crime, and leaving right away."

She elaborated on the number of Keyes's victims.

We believe there are eleven victims total, and that is based primarily on what Keyes told us. He was evasive. He was very evasive at times during interviews, and he told us when we tried to pin him down on a number that it was less than twelve. But then there were things that he would say that led us to believe that by "less than twelve" he simply meant eleven. He was quick to correct us in interviews if we had something wrong. There were several times where we just threw out statements like "your eleven victims" and things like that and he didn't correct us. So, based on that and some additional things that he said, we believe the number is eleven.

Goeden also emphasized that Keyes seemed to have an overwhelming urge to kill, an urge that continually kept him hunting for more victims.

"He talked about having the thoughts, having the urges to do it," she said. "He would commit a crime and that would satisfy that thought or urge for a while. And then it would come back again."

A national expert on serial killers retained for the case opined that Keyes was one of the top three organizers, thinkers, and planners out of all the serial killers he ever studied. And Goeden was fascinated by the degree of forethought that went into his crimes.

Keyes was very meticulous. His crimes were very well thought out. There was nothing that was spur of the moment or he just went out one day and decided to do something. Everything was meticulously planned, and our interviews with him were the same from his standpoint. I never got the sense that he accidentally told us something or got angry and riled up and something flew out of his mouth. My sense was that he knew every time he came in what he was going to give us that day.

The double-life that Keyes enjoyed became harder and harder to maintain as the urge to kill became increasingly difficult to satisfy. Although he "enjoyed the fact that he fooled people," he could not help showing his other side when talking about what he had done.

"There were times we talked to him and had a normal conversation, like you were talking to your next-door neighbor, Goeden observed.

"Other times when he was talking about his crimes, it was a different Israel Keyes, the other side he didn't think people would ever see."

That other side lacked any empathy for his victims.

"He had no remorse at all," Goeden explained. "He enjoyed what he did. He talked about enjoying what he did. He talked about the fact that had he not been caught, some of his future plans and what he would have done, which included continuing to do what he was doing, continuing to kidnap and murder people, so he had no remorse at all."

She credited the Texas Rangers and other law enforcement in Texas for their role in apprehending Keyes and saving an untold number of future victims.

"When we were looking for him, all we had was a type of car, no license plate, no physical description. He had future plans and things he was planning to do, and he would not have stopped. If we had not gotten him, he would still be out there killing people."

Kevin Feldis explained that investigators felt that they had built a good rapport with Keyes and were making real progress in getting information from him about other crimes.

"As of this week, we were still obtaining valuable information from Mr. Keyes," he insisted.

Feldis also mentioned that during dozens of hours of interviews, Keyes, "never showed any remorse for his actions." He opined that Keyes's motivation for murder could not be fully explained; it was something that investigators "will never really understand." And he added to Mew's comments about Keyes's concern for his good name.

"He was sensitive to being labeled a serial killer and not wanting those details to come out on account of family and friends. Sometimes he was more willing to discuss things and sometimes he wasn't, and that was really under his control," Feldis said. "He could stop talking to us any time he wanted to."

Goeden pointed out that Keyes's suicide was consistent with his desire for a speedy trial.

"He wanted to avoid a long trial, publicity, and the media. Ultimately, he wanted the death penalty and he wanted it quickly. He didn't want to sit in jail for a long period of time."

Although Keyes had referred to his cell as a "concrete paradise" in which he passed the time engaged in such trivial pursuits as solving crossword puzzles, he simply could not stomach the notion of spending the rest of his life behind bars.

Russo characterized Keyes as operating at a level "more evil" than anyone else he had encountered. He recounted how the usually calm Keyes would shiver with adrenaline and sit at the edge of his seat whenever he discussed murders that he had committed.

"He described that he had a fairly normal childhood and this was a proclivity that he always had, enjoying watching things suffer," Russo recalled. "It would be just like talking to one of us across the table, but it would be this person who had another side to him that enjoyed killing people. His only regret was that he didn't kill more people while he was out of jail."

Russo found himself being personally impacted by the case.

"Mr. Keyes said a lot of haunting things," Russo remarked reflectively. "And I thought I'd heard just about everything."

Anchorage detective Jeff Bell experienced a similar reaction listening to Keyes's confessions.

"When he was telling us details, he enjoyed telling us details. It was chilling to listen to him, to watch him."

And yet, despite his dark side, Keyes had exhibited genuine feelings of concern about his daughter.

"He was very conscious of his daughter Googling him years from now and having to deal with the fallout from this," Russo said. "This is a guy who really cared about his family."

Like his fellow prosecutors, Russo felt a sense of defeat in the wake of Keyes's suicide.

"I feel like we lost this case," he explained. "And we lost because we couldn't get these people out of his head that he kept there. That's how he described it. 'I have these people, they're my people, they belong to me.' In killing himself, that was his answer to us: 'You'll never get these people out of my head'."

Feldis echoed Russo's sentiments.

"There's a lot more out there that only Israel Keyes knows," he said. "And he took that to his grave."

Later, forensic psychologist Tom Powell described Keyes's suicide as "his ultimate power grab," his final act of control that kept investigators from learning about his other victims.

"He was able to hold back that information knowing the rest of us would have these questions exactly as we're asking them now," Powell said.

Although the Alaska investigators acknowledged that Keyes's suicide would detrimentally impact the investigation, they vowed to keep trying to find his other victims.

"There are still a lot of unknowns, unanswered questions for families out there," Goeden acknowledged. "It's really important to us to be able to bring some type of closure to family members that are still wondering what happened to their loved ones."

Rook echoed that sentiment.

"We're going to continue to run down leads," she promised, "so that we can bring some closure to the families."

Karen Loeffler agreed that, despite the unique challenges and complexity of the case, prosecutors would keep exploring leads.

"This has been massive," she said. "It started out massive with the Anchorage Police Department doing every possible thing they could to find Samantha Koenig under the hope that she was still alive. And it evolved into something even bigger when we found out what we had."

Although Loeffler found it difficult to ascribe a cause for Keyes's homicidal behavior, she was determined to keep working the cases.

"This isn't a concrete thing that somebody can answer," she said. "But even though Mr. Keyes is dead, our investigation continues."

The common denominator among all who had worked the case was that no one could say for sure what had led Keyes to kill.

"Everyone keeps looking for a push point where this guy went sideways," Russo commented, "but in my view, it seemed like he was born this way."

Russo pointed out Keyes's fascination with serial killers and his personal identification with Ted Bundy, a connection largely stemming from Bundy's ability to live a double-life much like Keyes himself. Russo had been surprised by Keyes's comments about another serial killer, Dennis Rader, the BTK killer.

"He described Rader as a wimp. He couldn't understand why he came out and said he was sorry for everything he'd done." Aside from Bundy, Keyes had most admired serial killers "who haven't been caught."

James Koenig was outraged that Keyes had been able to commit suicide prior to his trial.

"I'm not happy with it," he growled. "He just robbed Samantha of him standing trial and being convicted. The corrections department dropped the ball. He shouldn't have had anything in his cell that could be used to kill himself. He should have stood trial in front of everybody. It's just one more thing he robbed from us," he said bitterly.

Jacob Gardner, pastor and advisor to Keyes's mother, Heidi, conveyed the Keyes family's reaction to the news of his death. Gardner said that Heidi was grieving not just for her son's crimes and death, but also for the never-ending torment he faced in the afterlife. Keyes's lack of remorse and disinterest in forgiveness had condemned him to eternal damnation, his unrepentant soul sentenced to forever suffer in proportion to the extent of its wickedness.

"It's not something for carnal, wicked men to glory in, or rejoice, that he's burning in hell and such things," Gardner admonished.

"We're not glad that he's in hell. The family lost an eternal soul. They see the weight of eternity before their eyes, and so the grief is immense," Gardner stressed. "His mother sees that her son's life has been used greatly for the worst. It's been used greatly as a mockery of all that is good and right, all that is God. It's been a shame. It's an eternal soul they lost. There is no second chance."

Twenty-Seven

After the Alaska investigators spoke to the media about Keyes's suicide, Vermont authorities held their own press conference on December 3 in the federal courthouse in Burlington. Standing at a podium adorned with the Department of Justice emblem, and clad in a dark suit and spotted tie, the U.S. Attorney for Vermont, Tristram Coffin, gave a prepared statement to the press:

At about 11:15 yesterday morning, Alaska authorities informed us that Israel Keyes was found dead of an apparent suicide in the facility in which he was incarcerated in Anchorage, Alaska. Keyes had been detained since March on charges relating to the murder of 18-year-old Samantha Koenig of Anchorage, Alaska.

In the course of investigating Keyes' role in that homicide, investigators in Alaska became convinced that Keyes had committed other murders. During the course of multiple interviews with Keyes, he confessed to investigators in Alaska that he had murdered Bill and Lorraine Currier of Essex Junction, Vermont.

Since April of 2012, federal, state, and local authorities from Vermont have been working closely with Alaska authorities in investigating the Currier murders. Although searches in Essex and

Coventry, Vermont were unable to locate the Curriers' remains, investigators obtained enough details to confirm that Keyes did murder the Curriers.

Keyes also claimed that he had committed multiple other murders throughout the country. Efforts to investigate those murders have been ongoing and will continue.

Based on discussions between Keyes and investigators in Alaska, Alaska authorities requested that Vermont authorities not publicly disclose information linking Keyes to the Currier murders in an effort to further the investigations of other murders. Vermont authorities agreed with this request as the public was not at risk due to Keyes' incarceration and in the interest of identifying the victims of unsolved murders. The Currier family strongly supported efforts to identify other victims. We appreciate their courage and selflessness in wanting to assist other families who have suffered a similar unspeakable tragedy.

Coffin stressed that the Curriers had not done anything to cause Keyes to target them. They had simply been victims of circumstance.

"We wish to reiterate that the Curriers in no way did anything wrong or contributed in any way to this tragic series of events occurring," Coffin said. "By all accounts, they were friendly, peaceful, good people who encountered a force of pure evil acting at random."

Coffin also commented on the pointlessness of trying to understand a reason for Keyes's acts.

"He provided some motivation, but I don't think it's really possible to pigeonhole why he did this," Coffin said. "It was something that he could control and he liked to do it. Why someone likes to act like that, nobody knows."

Clad in a light suit and striped tie, Chittenden County State Attorney T.J. Donovan discussed Bill and Lorraine Currier's abduction and murder, careful to highlight the human element of the crime amidst the terrible details of the killings.

"It is clear from the facts of this case that, though confronted with death, Bill and Lorraine showed extraordinary bravery and an extreme dedication and love for each other," Donovan emphasized. "They fought to the end," he said emphatically.

Donovan reiterated the randomness of the crime, pointing out that the Curriers' home had simply fit the criteria that Keyes had in mind: a house with an attached garage, no cars in the driveway, no children, and no dog. The crime had been so random, in fact, that it produced absolutely no leads and no indication of having any link to the Samantha Koenig murder whatsoever.

Detailing Bill and Lorraine Currier's final hours, Donovan described how Keyes left the Handy Suites motel on Susie Wilson Road and walked a few blocks until he came to the Curriers' street. He considered several houses on the street until he decided that the Currier's home met his criteria. After watching the house and waiting for an opportunity to act with no witnesses around, Keyes cut the Curriers' phone line to make sure there was not an alarm system that would alert the police.

When no alarm went off after he had waited for several minutes, Keyes found a crowbar in the garage and used it to shatter the window of the door leading into the kitchen. Wearing a headlamp to provide lighting, Keyes conducted a "blitz" attack on the Curriers, making it to their bedroom within five or six seconds of breaking into the house. Having surprised the Curriers while they slept, Keyes tied their hands with zip ties, and then interrogated them about the house and their belongings.

He searched through the house and took several items, including the Curriers' cell phones and Lorraine's Ruger handgun that she kept for self-defense. He noticed the insignia of the Army's 25th Infantry Division in a drawer in the spare bedroom. Often called the "Electric Strawberry" due to the strawberry-shaped taro leaf with a lightning bolt emblazoned across it, the insignia led Keyes to learn that he and Bill Currier had both been assigned to the same Army division during their military service.

Keyes then forced the Curriers into their own car, still parked in the garage. He put Lorraine in the front passenger seat with her hands cable-tied behind her back and her feet cable-tied together. He put Bill in the back similarly secured. To keep them cooperative, he told them that they were being kidnapped for ransom and were being taken to a drop house where he would turn them over to his colleagues. Then he drove to the Handy Suites and picked up a shovel, trash bags, and two gallons of Drano, all of which he put in the trunk of the car. From there, he drove to the vacant farmhouse at 32 Upper Main Street, which he had previously chosen as the site for murdering whoever he abducted. After parking at the back of the building, he took Bill out of the car and walked him into the basement through a rear entrance. He strapped Bill to a stool with more zip ties, then left the basement to retrieve Lorraine from the car.

Upon returning to the car, Keyes discovered Lorraine standing next to it, having broken free from the zip ties that secured her hands and feet. When she saw him coming back, Lorraine turned and ran towards the road, but Keyes quickly caught up to her, tackling her from behind. He dragged her to a second-floor bedroom in the farmhouse and tied her to a mattress with duct tape. Using a nylon rope, he knotted a hitch around her neck and tied another rope to her left foot, fastening it to a 20-inch-long pipe that was attached to the wall under a window frame. He tied her other leg as well so that she was lying spread-eagled. As he finished securing Lorraine, Keyes heard noises coming from the basement.

Returning to the basement, Keyes found that Bill had broken free from his constraints to the stool. As Keyes descended the stairs, Bill began bellowing, "Where's my wife? Where's my wife?" When he refused to comply with Keyes's demands to shut up and sit still, Keyes grabbed a shovel and beat him with it. When Bill continued to struggle, Keyes went upstairs and retrieved his 10/22 gun and silencer. He returned to the basement and shot Bill Currier in cold blood, emptying the gun's ten-round magazine into his arms, neck, head, and chest. Still standing when the final shot was fired, Bill fell to the ground seconds later.

Having murdered Bill Currier, Keyes returned to Lorraine on the second floor. As he started cutting off her clothes with a knife, Lorraine realized what he was going to do and tried to fight him off, but he overpowered her. He pinned her flat on her back on the mattress and raped her. Then he gagged her with paper towels and duct tape, turned her over onto her stomach, and raped her again. During the second sexual assault, he strangled her, squeezing her neck with his bare hands until she passed out. After she regained consciousness, he took her down into the basement and sat her on a bench. He put on leather batting gloves, stood behind her, and strangled her to death with a rope. Strangulation had always been his preferred method of killing because he enjoyed watching his victims suffer. As a safeguard, he tightened a cable tie around Lorraine's neck to make sure she was dead.

Now he needed to get rid of the bodies. He placed Bill and Lorraine in separate heavy duty trash bags, using two bags for each of them to fully enclose their bodies. Next, he poured one gallon of Drano on each of them, being sure to saturate their hands, face, and chests. Then he tossed the bags in a corner of the basement, careful to cover them with garbage, wood, and other debris.

Having concealed the bodies, Keyes left the farmhouse and drove the Curriers' car to the Lowe's on Susie Wilson Road, just a few blocks away from where he had abducted them. He walked back to the Handy Suites and checked out of the motel at approximately 8:00 a.m., then drove his rental car to the Rite Aid on Suzie Wilson Road across the street from Lowe's. After walking to Lowe's, he drove the Curriers' car up Route 15, intending to rob several banks that he had previously staked out, but he only made it as far as the town of Johnson when he noticed that the car seemed to be overheating and that it was also nearly out of gas. Wary of breaking down, Keyes returned to Essex Junction and abandoned the car in the parking lot of an apartment complex at 241 Pearl Street. Then he walked back to his rental car and drove to Bangor, Maine, to visit his brother.

After leaving Maine, Keyes headed back towards Vermont, stopping at a national forest in New Hampshire to burn a suitcase full of the Curriers' belongings that he had stolen from their home. Upon returning to Essex Junction, he drove by the parking lot where he had abandoned the Curriers' car. It excited him to see that the area had been closed off by police crime scene tape.

Having satisfied his morbid curiosity, Keyes drove to New York via the Grand Isle Ferry, and eventually made his way to the reservoir in Parishville, where he tossed Lorraine's Ruger handgun into the reservoir, along with the barrel and bolt of his 10/22 and silencer, the gun he had used to kill Bill Currier. He subsequently drove back to Chicago and caught a return flight to Alaska.

Although Donovan had prosecuted countless cases involving horrific crimes, none of them had affected him more than the Currier case.

"They were good people," he said dejectedly, "and good people like that shouldn't have to die the way they did. They were good, hardworking, honest Vermonters."

Prior to the press conference, the Currier family was asked whether the details of what happened to Bill and Lorraine would be too difficult for them to hear. Marilyn Chates spoke up on behalf of the family.

"If Bill and Lorraine had to suffer through this, we can suffer through hearing about it," she said stoically.

Despite the news of Keyes's suicide, Bill and Lorraine Currier's former co-workers still struggled to come to terms with what had happened to them.

"There's some sense of closure in that he's not here any longer," said Jane Vizvarie, Lorraine's former manager at Fletcher Allen, "but it does make people feel a little cheated that he didn't have to pay more of a price." Lorraine's other colleagues at Fletcher Allen were still "too raw" to comment about the case.

"Lorraine was a really dedicated, hard worker," Vizvarie recalled. "Every single day, she was on time, working at her desk. She was the type of person you always want to hire. She knew her job well. She was fun and had a good sense of humor. She was very well liked. She was a wonderful individual."

University of Vermont veterinarian Ruth Blauwiekel expressed similar feelings on behalf of Bill's co-workers.

"That was a cathartic day for us," she said, remembering the memorial service for the Curriers held in August. "Bill was very conscientious, very professional. He helped train people. He knew how the equipment worked. He left behind a big gap in our institutional knowledge."

She also remembered how fearful the community had been during the months following the Curriers' abduction.

"People feared there was going to be another incident, another couple, another home targeted. It was very scary and sad. It's still scary, still sad, even though now we do know what happened."

Blauwiekel summed up the way that many residents' perspectives had changed as a result of what happened to the Curriers.

"There is bad in the world and there are bad people," she said wistfully, "and every once in a while, they intrude upon our lives, even in a beautiful place like this."

Paula Poulin, a nearby neighbor of the Curriers, still struggled to understand why Keyes had kidnapped and killed them.

"You don't know how to wrap your head around it," Poulin remarked disconcertedly. "Why somebody would do this is just beyond me. I just – I'll never get over it, I guess."

On the same day as the Vermont press conference, the FBI issued a press release through its Anchorage Field Office requesting the public's assistance in identifying additional victims of Keyes. Describing Keyes's "meticulous and organized approach to his crimes," the FBI release stated that he had committed "multiple kidnappings and murders across the country between 2001 and March 2012." In addition to the Curriers and Samantha Koenig, the release referenced four unknown murder victims in Washington and another victim in New York.

Although not stated in the release, investigators also suspected Keyes's involvement in a 1996 murder in Colville, Washington, where he spent much of his childhood. On March 3, 1996, five-foot one-inch, 115-pound Julie Harris, a twelve-year-old girl with prosthetic feet, disappeared after leaving her house. Julie had been born with a blood disorder that left her with scars and skin grafts and caused her lower legs to be amputated just below the knees. She had awakened early that morning and dressed quietly in her bedroom surrounded by the many Special Olympics medals that she had won, including a gold medal for downhill skiing. She grabbed four slices of pizza, told her mother goodbye, and headed out the door. She was never seen alive again.

A little more than a month later, on April 15, Colville police announced that Julie's artificial legs had been discovered at the mouth of the Colville River where it flows into Lake Roosevelt near Kettle Falls. However, there was no other trace of her to be found.

A year later, on April 29, 1997, a group of children playing along a rural road outside of Colville stumbled across skeletal remains in a wooded area near Haller Creek Road and Reidel Creek. Dental records positively identified the remains as those of Julie Harris.

A childhood friend remembered how Julie loved to challenge people by telling them that she could walk without her prosthetic legs. She loved to see the looks of disbelief on their faces when she proved herself right, and in the process showed them how she refused to let the loss of her legs diminish her spirit.

Colville police were baffled by Julie's murder. At the time, they had no reason to suspect eighteen-year-old Israel Keyes who lived just outside of town.

Jeff Bell acknowledged that, although Keyes admitted to committing eight murders, he had also indicated that there were "a lot more."

"We don't have a number, we just believe it's more than the eight,"

Bell disclosed. "What we are trying to get is closure for these families. He didn't feel that same moral obligation, and he told us that in so many words."

Jolene Goeden agreed, emphasizing that investigators would continue to work the case.

"We still have a lot of work ahead of us," she acknowledged. "This case is a little different from other serial killer cases, where typically you would find a number of victims and try to connect them back to a person. In this case, we have the person and we're trying to find the victims."

The next day, December 4, Kevin Feldis emailed Mary Morrissey to advise her about how much detail she could divulge to the media about the Currier case in light of the confidentiality requirements of the grand jury proceedings in the Samantha Koenig case. Although the criminal case against Keyes was "effectively over" due to his death, Feldis cautioned that they "still must respect the secrecy of the grand jury process." He suggested that Morrissey exercise discretion in talking with the media, reminding her that the "number one thing, of course, continues to be to try to solve other crimes Keyes has committed." In closing, Feldis expressed his appreciation for the Currier family's cooperation in not disclosing Keyes's connection to Bill and Lorraine's murders. He acknowledged that their "cooperation, understanding, and sensitivity was very important" in enabling federal investigators to obtain "valuable information" about Keyes's other victims.

Twenty-Eight

A t a December 10 press conference in Anchorage, Monique Doll described her belief that Keyes chose to confess the murder of Samantha Koenig to her because she had told him shortly after his arrest that killers were made, not born.

"I think based on our subsequent contact with him, he kind of wanted to look me in the eye while he told me about Samantha," Doll said. "I think he wanted to prove me wrong – to show that monsters aren't created, they're born."

And it seemed that her interactions with Keyes had altered her original opinion.

"Israel Keyes didn't kidnap and kill people because he was crazy," she concluded. "He didn't kidnap and kill people because his deity told him to or because he had a bad childhood. He did this because he got an immense amount of enjoyment out of it, much like an addict gets an immense amount of enjoyment out of drugs. In a way, he was an addict, and he was addicted to the feeling that he got when he was doing this."

She was struck by Keyes's confident – at times cocky – manner in discussing his crimes.

"I would describe him as extremely confident that no one would ever have connected him with any of these crimes, and that no one would have ever thought that he was capable of doing this."

Ironically, for someone who so valued control, it was Keyes's loss of self-control that ultimately proved to be his undoing. The crime that led to his arrest, the Samantha Koenig abduction and murder, had begun with clear parameters in his mind. As he approached the Common Grounds coffee stand that cold February night, Keyes had told himself that if the girl working in the stand did not have her own car, he would simply rob the store and leave. He knew that it would be too risky to abduct her using his own truck. But when he stood at the coffee stand's window and saw the teenaged Samantha Koenig standing alone inside, he could not stop himself.

"In prior cases, he had enough self-control to walk away from it, to not commit the kidnapping, to not commit the abduction, and with Samantha he didn't," Doll elaborated. "He broke his own rule. He had drawn his line in the sand and he couldn't help himself. He took her anyway.

His self-control, his ability to keep his dark side in check, was steadily diminishing. He continually needed the rush of killing for new stimulation."

Jolene Goeden also noted Keyes's steadily weakening self-control.

"He talked about that urge, that urge to go out and commit a murder," she said. "It was there and it would build. It would build over time between crimes. And it would build to the point where he would need to go out and do it again."

Though it never lasted for long, he derived immense pleasure from feeding his addiction.

"He definitely enjoyed it," said Goeden. "He never expressed any remorse for what he did. It wasn't anything he was embarrassed about or remorseful of or ashamed of. He enjoyed it."

But throughout hours and hours of interviews siting across the table from him, Doll found it particularly interesting that Keyes had not wanted to be considered a serial killer, despite the fact that he admitted kidnapping and killing at least eight people over a span of more than a decade.

"He had researched and read other serial killers. For example, he knew a lot about Ted Bundy," Doll recalled.

As far as him researching other serial killers, he did have a lot of interest in books about other serial killers, and suspense crime movies and books and things of that sort. But again, he was very realistic and said, "You know, it interested me because I couldn't talk about it, but that's what I was. I recognized that likeness, I recognized that sameness."

But he was very careful to say that he had not patterned himself after any other serial killers, that his ideas were his own. He was very clear about that distinction. That mattered a lot to him. He never identified himself as a serial killer. That was one of the things that he wanted very much to keep from being identified as.

On the same day as the Anchorage press conference, a light snow fell in Deer Park, Washington, during a small, subdued funeral service for Israel Keyes. Too disturbed by the secrets he had hidden from her, and too disgusted by his crimes, Tammie Hawkins had refused to accept his body for burial at Neah Bay. And in contrast to the large memorial ceremony in remembrance of his last known victim, Keyes's service at Lauer Funeral Home was so sparsely attended that aside from the pastor only his mother, four sisters, and three brothers-in-law were in attendance.

Church of Wells Pastor Jake Gardner gave a scathing sermon in the funeral home's chapel, emphasizing that Keyes would suffer in Hell for all eternity for his wicked acts.

Referring to Keyes's body as a "vessel of clay before us," Gardner made clear what he deemed to be Keyes's just reward.

"Do I believe that this man is in heaven? No. This man was not only a murderer of others, but a murderer of himself most of all. This man was cast into a cold sea of eternity where he will be forever without intermission, without hope. For eternity this man cast off the presence of God, and he is there now abiding an everlasting fire."

Gardner recounted how he had first met Keyes's family in November 2009 in Indiana, and how in March 2011 Keyes's three oldest sisters came to the Church of Wells to be saved. Their mother, Heidi Keyes, joined the church soon afterward. Gardner noted that after killing the Curriers, Israel had stayed overnight with his family in Indiana on his way back to Chicago. During that one-night stay, his sister, Sunshine, spoke to him about her religious faith, which had caused him to openly weep, but he remained steadfast in declaring his atheism. Keyes's next visit with his family had been in March 2012, just prior to his arrest, when he had debated with his sisters' husbands about God, while they tried to convince him to renounce his sinful ways. Despite his sister's assurance that God would forgive him regardless of whatever sins he had committed, Keyes had rejected her offer of assistance and denied the existence of such a divine power of forgiveness.

Gardner spoke about Keyes's "conflict of conscience," referring to the "second person who he had always been" and pronouncing that he "lived a lie for fourteen years of his life," a time period during which "no one knew who he was."

Despite his family's enduring feelings of love for him, Gardner said, they were well aware of the "fearful reality that this man is in Hell."

After reviewing a tape of the Anchorage press conference the next day, George Murtie made an addition to his case report.

> Jeff Bell comments on how [WCAX-TV's] story shut Keyes down for two months. Keyes found out about the story by them telling him about it. Bell says that Keyes shutting down and their time spent having to rebuild rapport with him explains their failure (my words)

to get any more specific information from him before he killed himself.

It was interesting to learn that Bell and Doll had the luxury of being allowed to travel to TX and interview Keyes after TX authorities had captured him. Apparently, this set the groundwork for much of their ability to talk to him once he returned to AK.

Murtie also noted that Keyes's behavior leading up to the Currier and Koenig murders showed that he was "becoming more impulsive and compulsive," particularly since he was "actively looking for victims in his own backyard."

Like many others, Murtie experienced alternating reactions of anger and disappointment that Keyes had killed himself. He felt that Keyes's suicide was a crime against society as well as a crime against the families of his victims. Murtie wanted to see Keyes receive justice through the judicial process, but he reminded himself that Keyes would face justice in the afterlife.

———

On December 12, the Texas Department of Public Safety honored Corporal Bryan Henry of the Texas State Troopers and Texas Ranger Steven Rayburn for their roles in apprehending Israel Keyes. In addition to being honored at a Public Safety Commission meeting, both officers received a special letter of recognition from the Chief of the Anchorage Police Department.

———

Meanwhile, George Murtie continued to struggle to understand Keyes's motivations for killing two people he had never met or even seen before. Murtie was also amazed by Keyes's brazenness in abducting them from their house considering the character and make-up of the neighborhood.

"When you look at how close the houses are together, the risk that he was taking in selecting that house is just phenomenal," Murtie said. "He must have had a compulsion to do this that he couldn't ignore, and he figured he's smarter than everybody else so he could do it and get away with it."

That compulsion was what had eventually led to his capture.

"He was over-confident, and he got caught," Murtie commented before adding, "He would have killed again had he remained free."

Murtie's thoughts turned to the countless hours he had spent working the case trying to find that one bit of evidence that might lead to the safe return of the Curriers.

"An investigator's worst fear is that you have the key to solving the case right in front of you, and you ignore or overlook it. I wish that we could have returned Bill and Lorraine's remains to their family," he sighed, his eyes filled with intensity but also sorrow. "It didn't work out that way for any number of reasons, but there's only one person I'm holding responsible for that."

Twenty-Nine

J ust before the New Year, on December 30, the United States Attorney's Office dropped all charges against Israel Keyes pursuant to a motion filed by federal prosecutors declaring the indictment against him "abated by his death."

On January 31, 2013, local Fox news affiliate, Vermont Channel 44, aired *Cracking the Case*, a special report about the Currier investigation, as its lead story on the 10:00 news. A reporter presenting the story asked Murtie about his experiences working the case.

"Nothing about this case has been simple or straight- forward," he told her.

"Did anything you find really help with the investigation?" the reporter asked.

"No," Murtie replied without hesitation.

The reporter's questions turned to Murtie's difficulty in having to break the news to the Currier family that their loved ones were dead and that their bodies could not be recovered.

"These were all really nice people who the investigators that worked the case became attached to," Murtie stated. "It was an incredibly hard meeting, but it's such a wonderful family that they took the information as best as anyone could."

The next day, a friend of the Koenig family wrote a letter to the editors of the *Alaska Dispatch* newspaper, taking the paper to task for its continued coverage of Israel Keyes.

> Enough! Feb. 1 is the anniversary that Sam was stolen from us. Why must you continue to write about this horrendous, deviant spawn of Satan, selfish, narcissistic, pathological liar. As a society, we have become immune to such horror. As for blatant insinuations as "*It takes a long time to strangle someone*" and other grotesque statements, it's needless pain for Sam's family. The whole truth will never be known, as his "suicide circumstances" will never be revealed.

On February 6, the FBI announced that a suicide note had been found in Keyes's prison cell alongside his body. Handwritten in cursive with pencil on yellow legal pad paper, the four-page note was crumpled and soaked with Keyes's own blood. Indeed, the note had been so saturated in blood that the hand writing was illegible, and it had to be sent to an FBI laboratory in Virginia for restoration before the contents could be reviewed and analyzed. Even after meticulous restoration, part of the note was still unreadable.

It appeared that the note had originally begun with the line "Of life's most basic elements, you have completely lost sight," but Keyes had drawn a line through that sentence and instead began with "Global overuse, as you over-colonize" before continuing on:

> Where will you go, you clever little worm, if you bleed your host dry?

Back in your ride, the night is still young, streetlights push back the black in neat rows. Off to the right a graveyard appears, lines of stones, bodies molder below. Turn away quick, bob your head to the seat, as straight through that stop sign you roll loaded truck with lights off slams into you broadside, your flesh smashed as metal explodes.

You may have been free, you loved living your lie. Fate had its own scheme, crushed like a bug you still die.

Soon, now, you'll join those ranks of dead or your ashes the wind will soon blow. Family and friends will shed a few tears, pretend it's off to heaven you go. But the reality is you were just bones and meat, and with your brain also died your soul.

Send the dying to wait for their death in the comfort of retirement homes. Justify, say 'it's for the best,' it's best for you so their fate you'll not know. Turn a blind eye back to the screen, soak in your reality shows. Stand in front of your mirror and you preen, in a plastic castle you call home.

Land of the free, land of the lie, land of scheme Americanize! Consume what you don't need, stars you idolize, pursue what you admit is a dream, then it's American die.

Get in your big car, so you can get to work fast, on roads made of dinosaur bones. Punch in on the clock and sit on your ass, playing stupid ass games on your phone. Paper on your wall, says you got smarts. THAT TEST that you took TOLD YOU so, but you would still crawl like the vermin you are, once your precious power grids blown.

Land of the free, land of the lie, land of the scheme, Americanize!

Now that I have you held tight I will tell you a story, speak soft in your ear so you know that it's true. You are my love at first sight, and though you're scared to be near me, my words penetrate your thoughts now in an intimate prelude.

I looked in your eyes, they were so dark, warm and trusting, as though you had not a worry or care. The more guileless the gaze, the better potential to fill up those pools with your fear.

Your face framed in dark curls like a portrait, the sun shone through highlights of red, what color I wonder, and how straight will it turn plastered back with the sweat of your dread.

Your wet lips were a promise of a secret unspoken, nervous laugh as it burst like a pulse of blood from your throat. There will be no more laughter here.

I feel your body tense up, my hand now on your shoulder. Your eyes looking for a way out of this small dark room, forget the lady called luck, she does not abide near me for her powers don't extend to those who are deceased.

Precious pet, would that I could keep you, let you be the master of your own fate. What else, I wonder, would you willingly stoop to knowing full well what's at stake. My pretty captive butterfly colorful wings my hand smears, would I somehow repaint them with punishment and tears.

Violent metamorphosis, emerge my dark moth princess. I would come often and worship on the altar of your flesh. You shudder with revulsion and try to shrink far from me. I'll have you tied down and begging to become my Stockholm sweetie.

Okay, talk is over, words are placid and weak. Back it with action or it all comes off cheap. Watch close while I work now, feel the electric shock of my touch, open your trembling flower, or your petals I'll crush.

In releasing the contents of the note, the FBI stated that it had found no hidden codes or secrets in Keyes's final words, and deciphered no clues or information about the identities of his unnamed victims.

| Suicide Note (FBI Files)

On February 8, Kimberly Anderson listed for sale the 2456 Spurr Lane house that she had shared with Keyes. The asking price was $353,500. The listing described it as a "classic Turn-again home" with a master bedroom and – thanks to Keyes – a "totally customized bathroom with separate tub and walk in closet," a kitchen "surrounded by windows for natural light," and a living room with a "wood- burning stove and bamboo flooring." Whether or not the buyer realized that a serial killer had lived in the house and that a murder had been committed in a shed that once stood next to it, the house promptly sold just three months later.

Thirty

On May 14, James Koenig appeared on National Public Radio's show, *All Things Considered*. NPR reporter Daysha Eaton described him as a "burly man with icy blue eyes" before asking about Samantha.

"I miss her laugh and her smile and her eyes and hearing 'Daddy' come out of her mouth," Koenig said, he anguish still palpable in his voice. "That's the hardest part of my days anymore . . . waking up and reliving it every day in the hopes it's a nightmare, and she's going to come walking through the door any minute."

Eaton also interviewed Jeff Bell, who discussed the difficulties and frustrations of the Keyes case, including having to use multiple missing persons databases administered by state, county, and local governments.

"I remember getting the list of missing people, and it was depressing because there was a printed stack of papers that was at least three inches thick. You always feel like you've missed something or that there's going to be an obvious clue that stands out that we missed," Bell said disappointedly, echoing recent comments by George Murtie.

On August 12, the FBI released a supplemental statement requesting the public's assistance in its attempts to identify other victims of Israel Keyes. During the months following Keyes's suicide, the agency had pursued countless leads, but none of them led to the recovery of another victim. Having exhausted all other avenues of investigation, the FBI called the release "our last best hope of identifying victims." Keyes's eleven victims were believed to be male and female, ranging in age from late teens to the elderly. The release included a timeline spanning the 1990s to early 2012, including Keyes's first, unknown murder victim during the period of July to October 2001, an unidentified couple in Washington between 2001 and 2005, two separate victims between 2005 and 2006 disposed of in a Washington lake, and a female victim whose body he buried in upstate New York. The release elaborated on the extent of Keyes's crimes:

> Keyes admitted responsibility for robbing several banks during this time frame, two of which investigators have corroborated. Keyes used the proceeds from his bank robberies to pay for his travel, along with money he made as a general contractor. Keyes also admitted to traveling to various locations to leave supplies he planned to use in future crimes. Keyes stated he buried caches throughout the United States. The FBI recovered two caches buried by Keyes—one in Eagle River, Alaska, and one near Blake Falls Reservoir in New York. The caches contained weapons and other items used to dispose of bodies. Keyes indicated the other caches he buried throughout the U.S. contain weapons, money, and items used to dispose of victims.
>
> Investigators believe Keyes did not know any of his victims prior to their abductions. He described several remote locations that he frequented to look for victims—parks, campgrounds, trailheads, cemeteries, boating areas, etc. Keyes also admitted to frequenting prostitutes during his travels, and it is unknown at this time if he met any of his victims in this manner. Keyes indicated the victims are male and female and range in age from late teens to the elderly. Keyes told investigators prior to the murder of Bill and Lorraine Currier in Vermont, his victims' disappearance received little if any media

coverage. Investigators believe Keyes is responsible for 11 homicides. Keyes stated his murders occurred in less than 10 states but did not disclose all of the locations. Keyes described crossing into multiple states during the abduction, murder, and disposal of a victim. It is not unlikely that in some cases Keyes abducted a victim from one state, transported the victim to another state where he or she was murdered, and potentially drove the victim to a third state to dispose of the body. Keyes admitted to burglarizing 20 to 30 homes throughout the United States and talked about committing arson as a means to cover up a homicide.

The release also referenced a female victim with "pale skin" who was driving an "older car" at the time of her abduction, and a victim whose body Keyes had staged so that it would appear the victim died of accidental causes.

Jolene Goeden spoke about the FBI's rationale for issuing the new release.

"He gave us a number of clues. He talked openly about some of the homicides, but much of what he said only hinted at the things he had done. So we are trying to get information out there about what he did tell us. We are letting the public know the types of cars he rented, towns he visited, campgrounds he frequented. Anything that might spur someone's memory could help us."

Meanwhile, Keyes's crimes and suicide received extensive media coverage. On August 28, Nancy Grace devoted a segment of her show to *Israel Keyes: The Mind of a Serial Killer.* Grace discussed the eleven victims that law enforcement felt confident enough to officially cite, while also mentioning an unofficial projection that Keyes had killed "many, many more, possibly into the 30s, 40s, or 50s." Referring to Keyes's "murder kits" as a "particularly chilling detail of his modus operandi," Grace also discussed Keyes's perspective of viewing the entire country as "one vast hunting ground."

The next day, Dr. Drew covered the story on CNN using the title, *Israel Keyes: Father by Day, Killer by Night?* During the show, Casey Jordan, a criminologist, emphasized the lack of a set pattern in Keyes's method of finding victims, concluding that it was that very randomness which had enabled him to go on killing for as long as he had without being caught.

Drew also spoke with Jacob Gardner, the Church of Wells pastor who presided at Keyes's funeral, who commented that Keyes's mother had mentioned noticing "some troubling signs" from him during his childhood, though Gardner also stressed that the signs were "actually very limited."

"Growing up, there wasn't much to be seen until about the age of 15," Gardner noted, when Keyes started tuning in to different radio stations and different things."

Cheryl Arutt, a psychologist, ended the show with the observation that the Keyes case "shows us that we never really know who we're dealing with, that there are some people out there who look and seem normal on the outside, but who really have something terrible going on."

The following day, August 29, CNN's Jane Velez-Mitchell addressed the case as well, with one contributing reporter remarking that Keyes "may have been the most methodical killer in the modern age." Discussing the inconsistent profile and absence of an identifiable pattern among Keyes's murder victims, the reporter commented that "basically anybody could be a victim of Israel Keyes. That's what makes this case so scary. That the monster really could be out there next door."

Just over a week later, on September 8, FOX News's *On the Record* program joined the media frenzy by airing a story on the Currier murders. The show's host, Greta Van Susteren, introduced the segment by calling Keyes "more than just a cold-blooded killer," because of the extensive planning he employed in perpetrating his crimes. George Murtie appeared on the program to show Van Susteren sites in the Essex area relevant to the case, including the site of the murders and the location where Keyes had buried his kill-kit in the 68

Acres park area.

The day before Halloween, *Maxim* magazine ran a story entitled *American Monster: The Hunt for Serial Killer Israel Keyes.* James Koenig, described in the article as a "long-haired biker in a Harley Davidson shirt," explained his reason for agreeing to be interviewed for the story.

"I don't want other families to have to go through this," he said. "There's no manual on what you do when your child is missing or your family member is missing. I had to learn the hard way."

Keyes' cache in New York was stowed in a watertight bucket. Materials inside included a .22-caliber Ruger weapon without a stock, empty magazines, ammunition, and a silencer. (FBI Files)

In early November, the FBI released an updated timeline of Keyes's travels that it had compiled using receipts and rental car and flight reservation records. Several trips that Keyes took raised red flags as likely killing opportunities. In February 2004, Keyes had rented a car in Salt Lake City that he kept for seven days, putting 522 miles on it while traveling around the area, including the town of Logan, where he stopped at a Walmart. In July 2008, he drove through Utah and Wyoming, and bought a fishing license, a behavior particularly disconcerting to investigators because they knew that he had committed murders on other occasions in connection with fishing trips.

The FBI also released a statement identifying 49-year-old Debra Feldman of Hackensack, New Jersey, as a likely victim of Keyes. Feldman had last been seen on April 8, 2009, a time when Keyes was in the area, and Keyes admitted abducting a female on April 9 of that year from a state on the East Coast, transporting her across state lines into New York, murdering her, and burying her near Tupper Lake in New York. While being shown pictures of missing persons, Keyes had also paused when he came across a photo of Feldman, before stating that he was "not ready to talk about her yet."

A blog administered by Steve Huff referenced the Feldman case, calling Keyes "one of the scariest goddamned serial killers in modern times," the type of killer usually "only found in suspense fiction: intelligent, and resourceful to an absurd degree. Absolutely invisible."

In October 2014, Jim Clemente, a former FBI special agent, discussed the Keyes case on the television show, *Crime Time*. Clemente dubbed Keyes "probably the most sophisticated serial killer in recent times."

The fallout from Keyes's suicide extended beyond its damaging impact on the investigations of his unknown crimes. It also put the Alaska Department of Corrections under a microscope as the media and outraged members of the public demanded to know how Keyes had managed to obtain the razor blade used for his suicide. Facing intense scrutiny, the DOC seemed intent on finding a scapegoat, eventually firing five-year corrections officer Loren Jacobsen under the premise that he was talking with co-workers, reading a book, and using the

Internet while Keyes "managed to tie a noose around his neck and cut his wrist."

The Alaska Correctional Officers Association quickly came to Jacobsen's defense, producing evidence that, at the time of Keyes's suicide, Jacobsen was taking his mandatory break. Video recorded during the pertinent time period showed Jacobsen going on break at 10:05 p.m. and being relieved by another officer. Keyes could be seen in the video arranging items in his cell and getting into bed at 10:12 p.m. He seemed to be moving around under the sheets until a sudden jerking motion occurred at 10:24 p.m., after which time the movement stopped entirely. Jacobsen returned from break nearly a half-hour later at 10:52 p.m.

Jacobsen, in turn, accused the DOC of putting Keyes – who he described as a "pretty quiet prisoner" – in an improper cell that made it difficult for any corrections officer to effectively monitor him during the course of the night.

"It has a different type of window in it," Jacobsen explained. "It's actually a plexiglass. It's scratched and hazed, and that makes it hard to see through. Everything looks black and white because the cell is darkened."

According to Jacobson, the arrangement of the desk and upper bunk in the cell also contributed to the impaired view of Keyes's sleeping area by causing a shadowing effect on his bed. Perhaps most puzzling of all, after Keyes came off of suicide watch, he was put in a cell without an in-room monitoring camera.

Jacobsen had caught Keyes with a sharpened pencil and noose several months before his suicide, and he had been placed in a "suicide cell" in the mental health unit of the facility for a period of time, but he was eventually returned to the Bravo module, a maximum security unit housing long-term prisoners, and put in the cell in which he ultimately took his own life. When Jacobsen had inquired why Keyes was not in a cell better equipped to monitor him, he received a distressing response.

"I was told that, 'there's been a deal made and he's moved where he wants to be so that he will tell his story to the federal Marshals.'"

An arbitrator assigned to review Jacobsen's firing found that he had been wrongfully terminated because he could not have reasonably been expected to prevent Keyes's suicide. The arbitrator concluded that Keyes had been "chillingly methodical and clever in completing his suicide."

As the weeks and months came and went, the FBI's timeline of Keyes's travels and appeal for assistance generated a significant number of tips from the public. In February 2015, Jolene Goeden revealed that more than 150 people had contacted the FBI about Keyes since August 2013 when the agency asked for the public's help in trying to identify his other victims. However, none of those contacts had resulted in any substantial and relevant information.

"We don't have any cases right now that we have any evidence that he is responsible for a person's disappearance," the disheartened agent stated.

Goeden reluctantly acknowledged the status of the investigation.

"It's cold. Absolutely, unfortunately, it's cold at this point."

Epilogue

Although it is said that time heals all wounds, Tammie Hawkins still feels the sting of Iz's deception and still wrestles with the meaning of her relationship with him. Looking back, she wonders whether the man she believed to be so straightforward and honest had showed signs of secret or suspicious activities, signs that she simply did not pick up on at the time. She is disturbed by the fact that he had a cunningness she failed to see, and she still struggles to reconcile the kindness and good deeds of the man she thought she knew with the dark side he kept hidden from her.

"When he first died, I struggled to understand whether our relationship had been a sham. Had I just been duped the whole time?" she asks, baring the essence of her self-doubt.

Tammie has never visited Iz's grave. In fact, she does not even know where he was buried. However, if he was alive today, she knows what she would say to him.

"I'd say, 'I love you,'" Tammie asserts unabashedly, "'and thank you for everything.'"

She remains angry at Iz for what he did to her and Sarah, taking the easy way out and forcing them to deal with all of the fallout from his actions by themselves. Yet, her love for him endures even with the knowledge of his evil acts. In a way that she finds difficult to describe, she loves and respects him even more for being able to take care of Sarah when she could not, for exercising the self-control to go from the "extreme bad to good."

"I couldn't have done it," she says, the admiration in her voice unmistakable.

She regrets that Iz never told her about his unknown victims so that she could give some closure to their families, but she is not surprised that he refused to reveal the names to anyone else.

"If there was anyone he could have confided in, it would have been me," she insists.

Although he never explained to her what drove him to kill, Tammie believes that it was a combination of his parents' extreme religious views – which he viewed abusive – and the demons of his growing alcoholism. She knows that many may want to label Iz as a psychopath, but she is convinced that he was not. Despite everything, she believes that he genuinely loved her and Sarah.

Tammie's only son, Keaton Wayne Hawkins, committed suicide on June 30, 2013, at the age of 20. In the weeks leading up to his suicide, Keaton had been battling anxiety and depression. Iz had been a father figure to Keaton and Iz's suicide deeply affected him.

It had been Keaton who drove Tammie to the FBI's local field office so that she could listen to tapes of Iz's confessions to investigators. She only made it through a couple hours of the tapes before she had to stop. She could not stomach hearing his monotone voice discussing murders that he had committed in such a casual manner, as if he was simply talking about the weather. It made her physically ill to hear him laughing as he discussed specifics about the crimes. The tapes showed her a side of him that she never knew existed.

Sarah still struggles to come to terms with the fact that her father was a serial killer. The fact that her father kept a secret side of himself hidden from her is in many ways the most painful part. Tammie promised Sarah that she would tell her everything about her father, but warned that once she "heard the truth, she would not be able to un-hear it." Sarah has not been able to sit down and talk about Iz with her mother, and Tammie is content to wait until Sarah is ready.

James Koenig misses his daughter with every fiber of his being. He keeps her ashes in a double urn that he displays alongside a memorial in a cabinet in his room. When he dies, his ashes will be put in the other side of the urn so that they can be together again. Not a day goes by that he does not think about Samantha.

"I miss her friendship, and the hugs and laughs, everything," he says sadly. "She made me a better person."

As for the circumstances of Keyes's suicide, James does not believe the explanation provided by the Alaska Department of Corrections that his possession of a razor blade was accidental.

"I don't think it was mistaken at all," Koenig asserts with obvious outrage. "How do you mistakenly give someone in segregation a real razor blade?"

Regardless of what he perceives to be Keyes's cowardly end, James remains committed to preserving Samantha's memory, while helping others who have lost family members to violent crimes.

"Samantha's life will not be forgotten," he vows from the bottom of his heart. "She will live on and continue to help everyone she touched."

Hoping to assist other families with finding their missing loved ones, he founded the Facebook page, Seeking Alaska's Missing, named after his dearly departed daughter. The page emphatically proclaims that "no family should ever have to suffer the horror of not knowing where their loved one is." To date, Seeking Alaska's Missing has over 22,000 followers and has helped located countless missing persons.

Duane Tortolani no longer works at Suite 100, and he has gone through several different jobs since Samantha's murder. He lives with his current girlfriend and their child, and he spends as much time as he can with family and friends. He still thinks about Samantha from time to time, but he long since fell out of touch with James Koenig.

Shortly after Samantha's remains were recovered, Duane packed up all of his things and moved out of the Koenig house without telling James that he was leaving, or why. The truth was that he simply could not handle living there anymore, sleeping in Samantha's room with all of her personal belongings around, being constantly reminded of what he had lost. He tried calling and texting James to explain why he had left, but James never responded.

"James doesn't want anything to do with me," he says somberly.

Christopher Bird is back in North Carolina, working in the heating and air conditioning industry, trying to get his life back together. He is still recovering from the emotional ordeal he endured in Anchorage. He has problems sleeping at night and finds it difficult to trust anyone. But he also misses Samantha.

"I wish I could talk to her every day," he exclaims. "Samantha was really cool. She didn't deserve what happened to her."

His mother, Tammie Counts, still seeks peace in the aftermath of what happened to their family during the weeks Samantha was missing. Asked about Samantha's family, she pauses before answering.

"We're living our life," she asserts ambivalently, "let them live theirs."

The investigation into Bill and Lorraine Currier's disappearance forever changed George Murtie. It exhausted him physically and emotionally, and it tested the depth of his spirituality.

"It's the hardest investigation and the longest investigation I've ever been involved with in 28 years," he says without hesitation.

Now a Captain and Operations Commander at the Essex Police Department, Murtie is still deeply bothered by the fact that the Curriers' remains were never recovered, and he regrets that Keyes was not caught sooner. Although his office pursued hundreds of leads and thoroughly evaluated eleven persons of interest during its investigation of the Curriers' disappearance, they had all amounted to a maze of dead ends.

"Never in a million years would we have solved it if not for the Koenig case," Murtie acknowledges matter-of-factly. The FBI's original contention that the Currier abduction was "personal" in nature and committed by someone who knew them turned out to be wholly false.

"Everything the FBI told us was dead wrong," Murtie sighs. "We never considered a serial killer scenario because the FBI said the odds of that were so remote. Not even a 1 percent of 1 percent chance."

Although the pure randomness of the crime made it virtually impossible to solve, Murtie could not help second-guessing himself. After Keyes's suicide, he wondered whether he had properly handled the case. He worried that he could have overlooked something which would have pointed to a serial killer as the Curriers' abductor and murderer.

Seeking some insight or reassurance, he reached out again to Robert Drew at the FBI's Behavioral Advisory Unit. Perhaps aided by the benevolent touch of God's grace, Drew emailed a response that provided Murtie some much needed peace of mind:

Serial Murder is a relatively rare event, estimated to comprise less than one percent of all murder committed in a given year. A completely random victim selection, where the perpetrator has absolutely no prior association with the victims, is exponentially even rarer. And even in those cases, the victims tend to have higher risk levels than did the Curriers. Forcible home intrusion murders are rare events. Home intrusion/kidnap/murders of adults are rare events.

282 • DEVIL IN THE DARKNESS

Sexually motivated home invasion/ kidnap/murders of two adults is extremely rare. Sexually motivated home invasion/ kidnap/murders of randomly selected victims by a complete stranger are EXTREMELY RARE events. Thus, if the broadly defined "serial murder" is less than one percent of murders in any given year, what happened to the Curriers is a minute percentage of even that small number.

While grateful for Drew's reassuring words, Murtie remains baffled by the Anchorage Police Department's reluctance, and sometimes outright refusal, to cooperate with his department during the investigation.

"Getting information from them was like pulling teeth," he says with a tone of vexation evident in his voice. "They acted like it was a turf war, like they thought the Currier abduction was their case instead of ours."

The whole set-up had been strange, from the APD and FBI's secrecy to the direct involvement of the U.S. Attorney's Office in interrogating a suspect.

But most of all, Murtie is still struck by how "brazen" Keyes acted in killing the Curriers, breaking into an unknown house in the middle of an unfamiliar neighborhood and abducting two complete strangers. Keyes had a "high risk of being caught" and his apparent calmness in perpetrating the crime led Murtie to conclude that "it obviously wasn't his first time doing something like that."

Keyes was unique in his degree of depravity, unlike anything else Murtie has come across during his now more than three decades of police work.

"It was evil on a level I had never encountered before," he says wearily, his voice trailing off, his eyes staring toward the horizon as if searching for something indiscernible, something nebulous in the distance.

In the end, Murtie believes that the Currier case made him a better homicide investigator, and he draws comfort from the fact that his exposure to the evil of a serial killer ultimately strengthened his Christian faith.

Having reflected on his involvement with the Currier investigation and what he learned about Israel Keyes, Murtie points to an essential truth that the experience proved. For him, the case reaffirmed the fundamental, universal truth that no matter how predictable or secure life may seem, it is in fact inherently fragile and all-too-often uncertain.

He knows that much is made about the high intelligence of serial killers like Keyes, but Murtie brushes off such characterizations, noting that it does not take a great deal of intelligence to attack weak and unsuspecting victims. All that is needed is some planning and cunning, and a disturbed mind inclined to commit such depraved acts.

"It takes much more intelligence to choose to make the world a better place because of who you are and what you do," he asserts with an inspiring tone of conviction.

Murtie knows that it is the choices we make in life that define us. Our decisions determine who we are and what we may become. Israel Keyes made a lifetime of choices, culminating in a series of selfish decisions to indulge his inner demons, ending with a fateful choice to follow the devil in the darkness.

At the Coventry landfill where their remains were lost and forever interred, a memorial flagpole stands as a silent sentinel in memory of Bill and Lorraine Currier. It is a touching tribute from a family that deeply misses and does not forget them.

In Essex Junction, a family amusement center has opened at 48 Upper Main Street. Smiling patrons play mini-golf and novelty games while enjoying ice cream and sodas, oblivious to the horror that occurred nearby, less than two hundred yards away, late one June night.

A short walk down the road leads to an empty lot where an old farmhouse used to stand. Although nature has reclaimed the lot with an overgrowth of weeds, a small wreath, shaped into a cross, marks the site where the Curriers were murdered.

From time to time, someone adorns the cross with flowers.

Acknowledgments

Special thanks to George Murtie of the Essex Police Department (and his wife) for their assistance in recreating the facts of the Currier investigation and for sharing how the case so deeply affected them.

I am grateful to Tammie Hawkins for speaking with me candidly about her romantic relationship with Israel Keyes. She has been through a lot and is continuing to deal with the aftermath of that relationship.

James Koenig's willingness to revisit and share painful memories is also greatly appreciated. I hope that telling his daughter's story helps in some way in bringing him peace. In honor of Samantha, James administers a Facebook page called Seeking Alaska's Missing (SAM) that aids in finding missing persons.

My appreciation also goes to Heather Andrews, Duane Tortolani, Tammie Counts, and Christopher Bird, as well as others who experienced the events of this story first-hand, some of whom spoke to me on the condition that their real names not be used.

Thanks to RJ Parker Publishing for helping initiate my writing career.

I owe a belated thank you to E.C. who, once upon a time, kept me from descending too far into the darkness.

As always, thank you to my friends and family for all that they do, especially J.B.W., who was once again an excellent sounding board and proofreader. This has been another labor of love.

About the Author

JT Hunter is a true crime author with over fifteen years of experience as a lawyer, including criminal law and appeals. He also has significant training in criminal investigation techniques. When not working on his books, JT is a college professor and enjoys teaching fiction and nonfiction in his creative writing classes.

JT is the bestselling author of *The Vampire Next Door: The True Story of The Vampire Rapist John Crutchley* and *The Country Boy Killer: The True Story of Serial Killer Cody Legebokoff.*

You can learn more about JT and his other books at www.jthunter.org

Sources

1. Court filings from Case No. CR01-5166 (W. Dist. WA).
2. Court filings from Case No. 3:12-CR-00041 (D. Alaska).
3. Court filings from Case No. 3:12-MJ-00126 (D. Alaska).
4. Materials and interviews obtained from the FBI, Anchorage Police Department, and U.S. Attorney's Office, including interviews of Israel Keyes from 3/30/12, 4/1/12, 4/6/12, 4/12/12, 4/17/12, 4/30/12, 5/16/12, 5/24/12, 5/25/12, 5/29/12, 6/7/12, 7/26/12, 11/29/12.
5. Interviews of Teresa Ealey, April and May 2015.
6. Interview of Keyes family friend Jennifer Johnson (name changed upon request) 3/15/15.
7. Interview of Tammie Counts 3/13/15.
8. Interview of Christopher Bird 3/11/15.
9. Interview of Heather Andrews (named changed upon request) March 2015.
10. Interview of Duane Tortolani 3/18/15.
11. Interviews of James Koenig: 9/24/14, 10/7/14, and 10/19/14.
12. Materials provided by James Koenig regarding Samantha Koenig.

13. Common Grounds surveillance video 2/1/12.
14. Newspaper articles and blogs regarding Samantha Koenig case, Bill and Lorraine Currier case, and Israel Keyes: June 2011-March 2015.
15. Facebook postings regarding Samantha Koenig.
16. Keyes Construction webpage (accessed 3/13/15).
17. Video recording of Samantha Koenig Celebration of Life.
18. Audio recording of Israel Keyes funeral sermon.
19. Interview of Mary Morrisey July 2015.
20. Interviews of Linda Murtie: Feb – April 2016.
21. Interviews of George Murtie: Feb 2015 – May 2015 and Jan 2016 – Apr 2016.
22. Case file and investigation materials of George Murtie regarding Bill and Lorraine Currier case.
23. Interviews of Tammie Hawkins: 10/5/15, 10/6/15, 10/27/15, 11/8/15, and 11/25/15.

Made in United States
Troutdale, OR
03/12/2024

18375927R00184